PLAY TIME

BY MURRAY SCHISGAL

★

★

DRAMATISTS
PLAY SERVICE
INC.

To Joyce and Arthur B. Greene

PLAY TIME was presented as a staged reading as part of the U.S. West TheatreFest at the Denver Center Theatre Company (Donovan Marley, Artistic Director) in Denver, Colorado, on June 6, 1991. It was directed by Bruce K. Sevy. The cast was as follows:

ALLEN BIRMINGHAM .... Jamie Horton
TOMMY GLENVILLE .... Richard Cox
BECKY BIRMINGHAM .... Lianne Kressin
DESIREE BENITEZ .... Laura P. Vega
DAISY HAKIM-MUSTAFA .... Jodi Baker

CHARACTERS

ALLEN BIRMINGHAM In his 40s. A true city-dweller. Filled with anxiety, uncertainty, stress, self-doubt. His emotions are held tightly in the pit of his stomach.

TOMMY GLENVILLE In his 40s. Well-educated, precise diction. His is self-assured, confident. He has a cheerful disposition and a bright, dazzling smile.

BECKY BIRMINGHAM In her 40s. Presents herself as a strong-willed woman but on meeting resistance reverses herself. She finds humor and joy in life.

DESIREE BENITEZ In her 20s. A professional singer and dancer. Shapely, very attractive. Hispanic. Great energy and sexuality.

DAISY HAKIM-MUSTAFA In her teens. A professional ballet dancer. Beautiful. Graceful.

All the characters wear full-bodied white leotards. They change their accessories: hats, gloves, briefcase, pocketbooks and jewelry.

If the director is so inclined, he may costume the actors in street clothes.

PLAY TIME

ACT ONE

Scene 1

Allen Birmingham's office at the brokerage firm of Dean and Leibnitz.

TIME: Spring: a little before four o'clock in the afternoon. 1989.

AT RISE: A grainy wooden desk and matching chair.

All the furniture — not the props and costumes — are made expressly for the play: this is communicated to the audience by the obvious "stage-fakeness" of the pieces.

At the rear is a large screen: the Wall Street market quotations of the day appear on a moving ribbon of digital numbers.

We hear the clicking of an old-time ticker tape.

Allen is seated behind the desk which has on it a Quotron computer, a phone, a brown briefcase and a gray felt hat.

He is wearing a full-bodied white leotard, white shoes and no socks. He has on a wedding ring and an inexpensive black plastic wristwatch.

His back is to the audience, the telephone receiver pressed to his ear. He stares up at the screen.

ALLEN. *(Into phone.)* The market is up today, Mr. Thorpe. A devaluation of the dollar is really working to our advantage.

(A short beat.) Yes, Sir. The GNP and the federal deficit are negative factors but employment is high and the price-earning ratio of most stocks never looked more attractive. No, Sir. Right now the market is moving up nicely, nicely, very nicely. I recommend we purchase five thousand shares of Contech. There's talk of merger. We can sell your Ginny Maes and Fannie Maes, convert some of your mutuals and municipals ...

(A short beat; turns in chair to face audience.) Mr. Thorpe, I'm fully aware that your portfolio has decreased in value thirty-two percent since I became your broker. That you should even suggest that I'm not familiar with your portfolio gives me great, *great* pain. As I told you on many occasions, you want four, five, six, seven percent interest on your investments without any risk factor, then by all means you invest your money in Certificates of Deposit, Treasury Bills or Money Market Funds. *But....* But if you're looking to realize an interest return of ...

(Bangs desk each time he says a number.) ... ten! twelve! fourteen! eighteen! twenty percent or more! then I'm afraid you're going to have to take a small amount of financial risk and you will have to gamble, you will have to put your money on the line, you will ...

(Rises; paces; glances at screen every now and then.) Yes, Sir. I agree. At times the market will go down. But you look at it over the last ...

(A short beat.) You don't have to go on, Mr. Thorpe. Indeed the picture has changed. Japan and Germany have indeed gone on to the forefront and surpassed us in the marketplace. Yes, Sir. It is remarkable, positively remarkable how those nations rose out of the bitter ashes of military defeat to reign victoriously in the battle of modern technology.

(A short beat.) Sad indeed. Sad indeed. We've turned in a few short years from *numero uno* to the greatest debtor nation in the world. Last year we imported one hundred and seventy billion dollars more than we exported. It's astounding!

It's mind-boggling! Our budget has reached the trillion dollar market and we owe two-and-a-half trillion ...

(A short beat.) What's that? You want me to close your account? You prefer Certificates of Deposit, Treasury Bills and Money Market Funds? You *don't* want to gamble with your money?

(A short beat.) What's that? You have no faith in our country and the assholes who run it? Mr. Thorpe, there's no need for vulgarity!

(A bell clangs. The digital numbers grind to a halt on the screen: it is end of the trading day.) Yes, Sir. It's your prerogative. I won't say another word, that's my reputation. Consider it done. My very best to Mrs. Thorpe.

(He returns phone to cradle. He bows his head, shakes it in dismay, thinks a beat or two: what am I doing with my life? Sound: Wieniawski's "Polonaise in D" or some such tune. Allen raises his head, stares out at audience. He freezes for introductory bars of music. Then he moves in tempo with the first theme of music. He presses his felt hat down on his head, picks up his briefcase and moves out of the office. Lights fade to dark.)*

Scene 2

Lights up on area in Central Park.

SOUND: "Polonaise" continues without interruption.*

TIME: A short while later.

AT RISE: A "stage-fake" park bench.

On the rear screen a simple, uncluttered abstract design of various colors that suggest the essence of place.

* See Special Note on Songs and Recordings on copyright page.

Allen enters, D.R., walks along an imaginary path. He walks stiffly, in tempo, briefcase in hand, hat on head.

Entering U.L. is Tommy Glenville.

He also wears full-bodied white leotard and white shoes. His hat is a black homburg and he carries a cream-colored attaché case. He has on a diamond ring, a Roman coin ring, a wedding band, and a large, gold wristwatch.

He's blessed with a wonderfully charming smile; his laugh is infectious, uncomplicated.

He walks along an imaginary path, U. in tempo.
He passes Allen, turns to cross, mid-stage, from L. to R.

Allen does the same from the opposite direction.

In a moment they come face to face. Stop.

SOUND: music ends abruptly.

ALLEN. *(Points finger at Tommy; can't remember who he is.)* Ahhh ...
TOMMY. *(The same gesture; the same predicament.)* Ahhh ...
ALLEN. *(Snaps fingers.)* You're.... You're ...
TOMMY. Ahhhhhh ... *(Finally responds.)* Glenville. Tommy Glenville.
ALLEN. That's it! We ...
TOMMY. *(Snaps fingers.)* You're.... You're ...
ALLEN. Birmingham. Allen Birmingham.
TOMMY. That's right!
ALLEN. *(Slowly.)* Waaait a second.
TOMMY. *(Slowly.)* Hooold it now.
ALLEN. Just ...
TOMMY. It's ...
ALLEN. It's ...
TOMMY. We met ...

ALLEN. At John Dooley's cocktail party! *(They laugh happily, slap at each other.)*

TOMMY. You've got it!

ALLEN. That's where it was!

TOMMY. John Dooley's!

ALLEN. What a night!

TOMMY. Who can forget!

ALLEN. What fun! *(They turn to face the audience. They sing loudly, with emphatic movements, stomping their shoes like a couple of music hall Munchkins. Sound: musical accompaniment.)*

TOGETHER.

What fun we had!
What fun we had!
We played, we danced,
We skipped, we pranced,
We joked, we giggled,
Our behinds we wiggled.
What fun we had!
What fun we had!

TOMMY. People stopped to stare at us!

ALLEN. They couldn't believe what happened to us!

TOMMY. We carried on like two old buddies!

ALLEN. On their vacation without any worries.

TOGETHER.

What fun we had!
What fun we had!
We laughed, we boozed,
We sang, we snoozed,
In a room upstairs,
Like a hundred years.
What fun we had!
What fun we had!

TOMMY. John Dooley himself came over to us!

ALLEN. To say that he was jealous of us!

TOMMY. For having such a superlative time!

ALLEN. While others were sucking on slices of lime!

TOMMY. With nothing to say!

ALLEN. And nothing to do!

TOMMY. As we went on!
ALLEN. Having fun!
TOGETHER.

We had such fun,
That it was absurd,
And here we are,
Together again,
Singing and dancing,
And having fun!

TOMMY. Ha! Ha! Ha!
ALLEN. Cockadoodledoo!
TOMMY. Ho! Ho! Ho!
ALLEN. Kitchikitchikoo!
TOMMY. And here we are!
ALLEN. Together again!
TOGETHER.

Having fun!
Having fun!
Having!
Having!
Having!
Having!
Having fuuuuuunn!

(The song and dance ends. If the audience applauds, the actors should acknowledge it. They laugh, back-slap at one another. They sit down on bench, put their hats and cases beside them.)

ALLEN. You don't know how many times I thought of you; how many times I thought of calling you, writing you, knocking on your door and saying, "Let's get together. Let's hang out. Let's plan a weekend, a trip, a vacation, a drive to the country, the mountains, the ocean, and see what's really between us."

TOMMY. My thoughts to the letter, Al. I doubt if a month has gone by since we met, and that must be ... *(Glances at calendar wristwatch.)* ... five years and six months virtually to the day, that I haven't said to myself, "I wonder what that fellow Birmingham is doing; I wonder if I got in touch with him he'd take offense, think me too pushy, too forward, too much of an opportunist trying to cash in on a fortuitous meeting at John Dooley's cocktail party."

ALLEN. I'd never ... *(He notices Tommy kneading his hands, looking uncomfortable.)* What is it? Is anything wrong?

TOMMY. No, no. Nothing of import. I stopped smoking recently and it's been a bit of a struggle for me.

ALLEN. Say no more. I stopped smoking ... *(Glances at wristwatch.)* ... four year, ten months and ... ten days ago, and I'm still dying for a pipe full.

TOMMY. Unfortunately you can't argue with the evidence.

ALLEN. You certainly can't.

TOMMY. Apropos, I also cut down substantially on my alcohol intake. I jog three miles five times a week, my diet is restricted to fish, skinless chicken, fruit, grains, vegetables, and I eat a head of broccoli every day.

ALLEN. You've just described my lifestyle almost verbatim.

TOMMY. What's your total cholesterol count?

ALLEN. Two-twenty-nine.

TOMMY. High-density lipoprotein?

ALLEN. Thirty-eight.

TOMMY. You don't want your total cholesterol to be more than three-hand-a-half times your high-density lipoprotein count. You've got an imbalance there, buddy. I suggest you try three grams of niacin daily and a bowl full of oat bran with skim milk to correct it.

ALLEN. I will. Starting tomorrow.

TOMMY. *(Crosses left leg.)* I'm enjoying this conversation.

ALLEN. *(Crosses left leg.)* So am I.

TOMMY. It's surprisingly pleasant.

ALLEN. It certainly is.

TOMMY. Reading anything?

ALLEN. *(Not much of a reader.)* Ahhhhh ...

TOMMY. Let me recommend you give Whitman's *Leaves of Grass* another perusal. *(Recites with poet's voice.)*

> "You shall no longer take things at second or third hand, nor look through the eyes of the dead, nor feed on the specters in books,

You shall not look through my eyes either, nor take things from me,

You shall listen to all sides and filter them for yourself."

(Normal voice; emphatically.) For yourself. Trust no man's judgment. This above all, to thine own self be true. Powerful, inspiring stuff.

ALLEN. I'll read it. This evening.

TOMMY. Been to the theater lately.

ALLEN. *(Not much of a theater-goer.)* Ahhhhh ...

TOMMY. You're missing nothing. They've forgotten how to place the body in space. Go see what they're doing in modern dance. Sheer magic.

ALLEN. I'll go. Definitely. This weekend. *(Tommy whistles, bounces his crossed leg up and down. Allen does likewise. A few beats. Tommy stops whistling. Allen whistles a bit more; stops; embarrassed.)* Can I tell you a secret ... *(Hesitantly.)* ... Tommy?

TOMMY. Please.

ALLEN. As you know, I meet a lot of people in my line of work, but, regrettably, I don't have a single, intimate friend.

TOMMY. That's not uncommon.

ALLEN. You...?

TOMMY. Intimate friends? No. Not anymore. Acquaintances? By the thousands. Nowadays sustaining intimate friendships is virtually an impossibility. *(He crosses his ankles under the bench; folds arms on chest.)*

ALLEN. Why is that?

TOMMY. Social habits have changed. The nuclear family has replaced the community. Worse, we're all into ourselves, into fulfilling our trite, selfish, mean-spirited indulgences.

ALLEN. I agree. *(Imitates Tommy's posture; arms folded on chest.)* That's why it's so strange that in one evening we became friends.

TOMMY. Good, close, intimate friends.

ALLEN. How come?

TOMMY. We give. We're generous. We don't lie.

ALLEN. We don't.

TOMMY. It's not in our nature.

ALLEN. It's isn't.

TOMMY. You comfortable, Al?

ALLEN. Very comfortable ... Tommy.

TOMMY. Can I get you anything? A cold can of diet soda? A decaf expresso from the bar across the street? A bag of butter-free popcorn or an unsalted whole wheat pretzel, perhaps?

ALLEN. Nothing, thank you.

TOMMY. *(Sits upright.)* I want you to have this, my friend. As a token of my esteem. *(Hands him his own wristwatch.)*

ALLEN. *(Sits upright.)* It's ... beautiful. It's ... I ... *(Hands him his own wristwatch.)* Will you.... It's not worth anything, but ...

TOMMY. I'll treasure it my entire life. As far as I'm concerned, it's priceless. *(They slip on their gifts. Tommy crosses his right leg. Allen does the same.)* Forgive me for not asking sooner, Al, how's the little lady?

ALLEN. Much better.

TOMMY. *(Puzzled.)* Much better?

ALLEN. *(Looks about; not wanting to be overheard.)* Major surgery.

TOMMY. No.

ALLEN. *(Nods.)* Five years ago. Seven weeks after John Dooley's cocktail party. December 5th, 1983. It was a Monday we found out. At ten-fifteen in the morning. She.... She.... She had it.

TOMMY. And she's much better?

ALLEN. *(Wide grin.)* All better. Not a trace of it in over five years.

TOMMY. *(Applauds lightly.)* Bravo. Bravo.

ALLEN. It was a horrible, horrible ordeal, Tommy. A nightmare. We fell completely apart.

TOMMY. *(Pats Allen's thigh.)* There. There.

ALLEN. After she.... After ... the surgery.... There was a time, for years, when I woke up every morning and I looked ... I stared down at the bed, expecting to see the ... the sheets ... covered and ... drenched with ... with ... and ... and when I ... when my wife went into the bathroom, every morning, every single morning, I ... I ...

TOMMY. You don't have to continue, my friend.

ALLEN. *(Unable to stop now.)* I stood outside the bathroom

door, holding my breath, my heart ... listening, listening, expecting any second for her to start ... yelling ... because ... she saw ... something ... again ... on her ... on ...

(Turns to audience; somewhat calmer.) Can you imagine what it was like for her? For my wife? A woman of thirty-eight, with two young kids? Healthy every day of her life and then, looking down at her body one morning, proud and pleased with the texture of her skin, the tautness of her flesh, and then finding ... finding ... there! Right there! It was right there!

(Rises; moves D.; to audience — out of need, not convention.) I don't know what she was thinking, fantasizing. I don't have the faintest idea. But as I said, we, the both of us, fell completely apart; we weren't ... courageous. She cried. She had ... fits of hysteria, depression, paranoid behavior. She had to take drugs to knock herself out so she could get through the day. And I lived every minute of it with her. But differently. Strangely ... differently. So that, with time, in time, I became obsessed, consumed, victimized by an illness that my wife had been totally cured of.

(A deep breath.) Now I'm going to tell you something ... unbelievable. I've been married for seventeen years, twelve years before my wife became ... ill, and five years after. There's no comparison between the two periods. None. I don't even remember the first twelve years. It's like I'm Mr. John Smith and I'm living with a wife and two kids and I have a job and an apartment and.... It's a blur, a haze. I'm traveling 180 miles an hour in a speed car. I don't remember any of it.

(He paces.) But.... But after her ... her ... illness, there exploded, there ignited inside me such a ... a profound ... passion, such a shamelessly emotional and physical *need* for her ... that for these past five years I can't forget the most trivial detail of our life together. It's amazing. I'm like an *idiot savant,* incapable of forgetting ... anything, anything. A sound. A taste. A touch. *(Stops pacing; faces front; recites like a schoolboy.)* I took my wife home from the hospital on January 18, 1984. It was a Wednesday. It was snowing; there was about four inches of snow that day. The first night we could go out for dinner together was March 4th, 1984. It was a Sunday. The

temperatures were frigid that month. It was the coldest March since 1960. My wife wore a brown tweed jacket with a silver Victorian "Best Wishes" pin on the lapel. I wore gray slacks and a blue blazer and a white shirt. No tie. We went to an Italian restaurant on Second Avenue called Elio's. The maitre d's name was Guilano. He was born in Siracusa, Sicily.

(He turns, walks U. and sits down on bench. Tommy's left leg is crossed. Allen crosses his left leg. A beat. To Tommy.) I never told that story to anyone.

TOMMY. That's what friends are for, Al.

ALLEN. Thank you. *(Tommy crosses right leg. Allen follows suit.)* Here I've been talking only about myself. How's.... How's your wife.... Ahhhhh.... Melissa! I remember her as a highly intelligent, extremely beautiful young woman.

TOMMY. I divorced her, Al.

ALLEN. *(Reverses himself at once.)* With very peculiar habits.

TOMMY. Let me see, I divorced Melissa nee Upjohn Cartwright three years ago this August. Confidentially, the woman thrived on drugs and kinky sex.

ALLEN. I can't say I'm surprised.

TOMMY. She loved to wear black leather brassieres and black leather baseball caps.

ALLEN. *(Wide-eyed.)* Really?

TOMMY. And she loved to carry a long, black leather whip. Every chance she got she'd snap that whip of hers. What was frightening is that I'd be sleeping and suddenly, in the middle of the night, all the lights would go on and there she'd be, at the foot of the bed, snarling and snapping her whip viciously over my privates.

ALLEN. *(A short reflective beat.)* I couldn't be married to a woman like that.

TOMMY. Nor I. I paid her off handsomely and a year later I married Celia Celeste Patimkin Lombardi, a fairly well-known politically active bisexual.

ALLEN. *(A perplexed beat.)* Did you, uhhh, know she was ... bisexual before you married her?

TOMMY. Of course. That was one of her more attractive qualities.

(He crosses his right leg. A beat and Allen does the same.) The fact is, Al, I was in love with her sister, Desiree Duchamps-Delissia Benitez. But, unfortunately, Desiree ran off and married a Count from Albania, so out of pique and frustration, I married Celia Celeste Patimkin Lombardi.

(Glances at wristwatch; jumps to his feet.) Ah! I must be off. I'm late. I have a five o'clock appointment at The Sign of the Dove. *(Puts on hat; picks up attaché case. Allen does the same, on his feet.)*

ALLEN. Would it be presumptuous to ask you to have drinks with my wife and me this evening? Say seven at 925 West End Avenue?

TOMMY. Unfortunately I have a dinner date at Le Cirque.

ALLEN. Just drinks. My wife always says I don't make enough of an effort to initiate friendships.

TOMMY. Are you still a stockbroker at Dean and Leibnitz?

ALLEN. Fourteen years in June. I don't have to ask you what you've been doing. Your financial conquests are in the *Journal* almost every day of the week.

TOMMY. Seven-fifteen. At your place. Come, I'll give you a lift in my limo. *(Sound: Wieniawski's "Polonaise."* They both freeze for introductory bars. Then Tommy puts his arm through Allen's and they move off together, brightly, in tempo with the first theme of music. Lights fade to dark.)*

Scene 3

Lights up on the Birmingham living room: an Empire-style love seat, facing front; an armchair and hassock, angled; near it a rack with newspapers and magazines; newspapers and magazines are on the floor around the armchair; on the left, a wooden rocking chair, angled; a side table, rear, L., with telephone on it. All built "stage-fake."

* See Special Note on Songs and Recordings on copyright page.

TIME: A short while later.

AT RISE: On the rear screen abstract design suggesting place.

Becky Birmingham is seated in armchair, feet up on hassock. She wears white leotard, low-heeled white shoes, a gold wedding band. She is reading a newspaper, opened to double-page width, with great concentration, murmuring the words aloud, as if committing to memory what she reads.

SOUND: Rock music coming from offstage bedroom, R., rear.

BECKY. "We live in a strange time, indeed. The 80s are not much different from the 20s. The prohibition mobsters would be quite comfortable living in our city today. They would be much sought-after, wined and dined and entertained by our trend-setting hostesses. The socially prominent Mrs. Pepperdine is quoted as saying ..."

(Shouts at offstage bedroom, R. rear.) Will you lower the phonograph in there!

(The music stops immediately. She lifts paper, reads.) "The socially prominent Mrs. Pepperdine is quoted as saying, 'Particularly desirable at any festive occasion is the Wall Street financier who has been indicted for stealing millions from his clients or a well-bred, matronly career woman who claims she killed her lover because he was ignoring her for a younger woman. Others in high demand,' Mrs. Pepperdine went on, 'are ex-cons who have literary talent, ex-socialites who run East Side brothels, and ex-politicians who have been employed at a salary in excess of five-hundred-thousand dollars annually to lobby for foreign governments.'" Tut–tut–tut–tut.

(Sound: Marco, Becky's fifteen-year-old son, opens and slams shut his offstage bedroom door. Turns to watch her son as he moves across foyer, rear, offstage, from R. to L.) Marco, where are you going? Your father's coming home from work soon! Don't you have any homework to do? Don't you have to study for a test? Did you clean your closet? Did you call your grandmother?

Who are you seeing? Why don't you see Jeffrey Norton? He seems like a ...

(We hear the entrance door, L., opening and slamming shut. She knows that Marco has gone but is compelled to talk nonetheless.) You don't know how to take care of yourself. You don't know how easy it is to get hurt, to get sick, to be injured and maimed for life, a leg, an arm, an eye, a scratch that won't heal, a bump that won't go away.

(She rises; puts newspapers and magazines on floor into rack; tidies up.) More than anything I want you *not* to have pain, *not* to have grief. What I don't understand, what I will never understand, is when, exactly, you became so serious about life, when you, exactly, became so grim, under the weather, subject to depression and dark moods and sourness and without explanation stopped giggling and teasing and being mischievous and.... When did it happen to you? Was it my illness, my cancer? Did that fill you with dread and nightmares? It shouldn't. It shouldn't, my son. Everything has worked out wonderfully. It's gone, evaporated, disappeared. We'll never see or hear of it again. I'm sure of it. I'm positive. I'm confident. But you don't talk to me anymore. You don't tell me what you're thinking, feeling anymore. You don't ... hold me like you did ... once ... once ...

(Sound: Zoe, Becky's sixteen-year-old daughter, opens and slams shut her offstage bedroom door. Turns to watch her daughter as she moves across foyer, rear, offstage, from R. to L.) Zoe, where are you ... Zoe? Zoe?

(We hear the entrance door, L., opening and slamming shut. As with Marco.) Why can't you stay, Zoe, talk to me, listen to me, tell me something you're hiding from me, what you're planning, what you said to Nick last night, anything, anything. You never have time, patience, inclination. You say I'm your best friend but you don't tell me, confide in me, confess, communicate.... It's Nick, Johnny, Scott, Tony. It's a world of sweaty boys and quick squeezes in cars and movie houses and dark doorways. When did it happen, my sweetheart? When did you change from indifference to impetuosity, from "I'm not interested in him, Ma," to "If he doesn't call me, I'll die, I'll

simply die, Ma!"

(Laughs.) I remember when you were nine, ten, we had a very serious talk, and I said, I told you, a boy's penis when he's excited gets hard and stiff like a stick, like a bat, like a magic wand, and he puts this stick, this bat, this magic wand into a girl's vagina, and you stared at me, straight at me, with a pinched, creased-up face and you said, "Disgusting! How ... dis-gus-ting!"

(Laughs.) I'll never forget ... "How ... dis-gus-ting!"

(Laughs.) ... you said, with your face looking like a crunched-up potato chip. How you changed, my sweetheart; how quickly you changed.

(Sound: the entrance door opening and slamming shut.)

ALLEN. *(Offstage.)* Becky! *(No answer; louder.)* Becky!

BECKY. In here!

ALLEN. *(Offstage.)* Close your eyes and don't move! *(Becky does so, standing stiffly, robot-like. Allen enters, without hat and brief-case. He carries a bouquet of flowers. On tip-toes he approaches Becky, stands very close to her, holding the flowers between them. Softly.)* Open your eyes. *(Becky does so. He kisses her lightly but noisily on the lips.)*

BECKY. I am so lucky. So, so lucky! *(She hugs him, kisses him wetly and noisily all over his face; then moves to side table to put flowers in vase.)* How did it go today? What did you do? Did you have lunch with anyone? Did you speak to anyone interesting or bump into anyone unexpectedly? How is your stomach? Is there a backlash from the grilled shrimp last night? Do you have anything at all to tell me?

ALLEN. *(Sits in rocking chair; takes off shoes.)* I had the most amazing surprise of my life when I was walking home from the office. I met.... Guess who it was?

BECKY. I give up.

ALLEN. Tommy.

BECKY. Who's Tommy?

ALLEN. Guess.

BECKY. I give up.

ALLEN. Tommy Glenville. You remember. We met him at John Dooley's cocktail party before you ... before you ... *(Can't say "became ill"; drops it.)* You'll never guess what I did.

BECKY. You invited him to come up and have drinks with us.

ALLEN. How did you know?

BECKY. I put two and two together. *(Continues tidying up.)*

ALLEN. Anyway, he's coming over. Becky ... *(Excitedly.)* ... he drove me home in his limousine, with a chauffeur, and he gave me his gold wristwatch, as a present, as a gesture of friendship. We talked and talked ... I have to admit now, I've been wasting my time. I haven't been living a full life. I've been operating on half my energy, half my potential. Becky, I want you to get us tickets for the modern dance festival at the Joyce Theater; I want you to buy me a copy of Walt Whitman's *Leaves of Grass;* I want us to go to the MOMA to see the Paul Klee show and the Guggenheim to see the Juan Miro show. This weekend.

BECKY. That must have been some limousine ride.

ALLEN. I still can't believe I ran into him. Here we haven't seen one another in five years and right away we started talking and having fun and we were like two old intimate friends, buddies who met every day to spend a few hours together. Me and Tommy Glenville. Unbelievable.

BECKY. He's a lucky man to have met you because when it comes to talking and having fun there is no one in the world who is more witty and entertaining than you are.

ALLEN. Thank you. *(Rocks in chair.)* So. How did your day go? Did you have a date for lunch? How's your diet coming along? Your exercise program? Your visit to the shrink? the periodontist? the podiatrist? Where are the kids? Do you have anything to say that would be of particular interest to me?

BECKY. I have so much to tell you I don't know where to begin. *(She continues tidying up.)*

ALLEN. *(Waits a beat or two.)* Becky? *(No answer; she's retreated so deep inside herself that even if she heard him she's unable to respond. A slight edge of panic in his voice; louder.)* Becky!

BECKY. *(Responds matter-of-factly.)* The kids will be home for dinner. Zoe's probably out with Nick and Marco's out who knows where, he doesn't talk, he's in a funk, the world has let him down in some unfathomable way, and I honestly think he can use an analyst, a counselor, a guidance teacher. As for Zoe, forget it, fooorget it; her pants are on fire, her nipples are bursting at the seams, she's ready to run off for life with the first four-wheel drive that comes down the street.

ALLEN. *(Puts on shoes; rises.)* The important considerations are as follows: one, we must be supportive; two, we must show our love; three, we must physicalize our love by touching, patting, pinching, stroking, squeezing and hugging; four, we must be a visible source of ethics, morality, integrity, not by laying down the law, but by setting an example as to what is acceptable social behavior and what is not acceptable social behavior. And if we do all of that, then I'm hopeful that Zoe and Marco will eventually get married and have children and sooner or later we'll get a little happiness out of them.

BECKY. You're brilliant. Your power of analysis is astonishing. You get right to the heart of the matter.

ALLEN. Thank you. I still can't believe that Tommy Glenville is coming to have drinks with us. *(He leads her to love seat; they sit.)* Do you remember his wife from John Dooley's cocktail party? Melissa nee Upjohn Cartwright? Listen to this: she's a pervert, deeply into drugs and kinky sex. The stories he told me ... *(Becky is all ears; she loves gossip of any kind.)*

BECKY. What stories? What did he tell you? Don't leave anything out. Don't skip anything. Give me a full report.

ALLEN. *(Dramatizing it.)* She wore black leather brassieres and black leather baseball caps and she carried a long, black leather whip.

BECKY. Really?

ALLEN. And when he was sleeping she'd stand at the foot of the bed and snap the whip over his ... testicles.

BECKY. *Really?*

ALLEN. But he divorced her and married Celia Celeste Patimkin Lombardi. But here's the interesting part. Guess what his second wife is.

BECKY. A bisexual.

ALLEN. *(Awe-struck by her occult powers.)* How did you guess?

BECKY. I put two and two together. What else did he say

about his second wife, Celia Celeste Patimkin Lombardi? Are they compatible? Is he cheating on her? She on him? Is there another couple involved or a *manage à trois* or some dark, evil, unspeakable goings-on that we don't know anything about?

ALLEN. *(Moves to sit in rocking chair; takes off shoes.)* He didn't say. He did say, though, that he wasn't in love with his second wife but married her because he was in love with her sister, Desiree Duchamps-Delissia Benitez, who was, it seems, already married to some royalty from Albania.

BECKY. That is sick. That is sooo sick. *(Sticks her finger in her wide-open mouth and makes sound of throwing up.)*

ALLEN. You're not funny. The man happens to be a warm, compassionate, giving, sensitive human being.

BECKY. Sensitive? He's sensitive? Here he is married to Melissa Upjohn Cartwright who's into drugs and kinky sex, he divorces her and marries Celia Celeste Patimkin Lombardi, not because he loves her, but because she's bisexual and he loves her sister, Desiree Duchamps-Delissia Benitez who's already married to royalty from Albania which to me is totally off-the-wall *sicko-wacko!*

ALLEN. There! There! You're doing it again?

BECKY. *(Apprehensively.)* What? What am I doing?

ALLEN. Every time I come close to making a friend, you become ultra critical; you have to put him down.

BECKY. I don't ...

ALLEN. Yes, you do. No wonder I have no friends.

BECKY. Not because of me. I'm always pushing you to have friends. You're the one who doesn't know how to develop friends, keep friends, how to further and nurture a relationship.

ALLEN. And you do?

BECKY. Yes, I do.

ALLEN. Then how come *you* don't have any friends?

BECKY. Ahhhhh.... Ahhhhh ... *(Rebounds.)* Honey, you are so unbelievably intelligent, so astute and multi-faceted that people should be kissing your ass to be your friend, that's all I'm saying.

ALLEN. I ... I like Tommy Glenville. *(Puts on shoes.)*

BECKY. I won't ever, ever say a critical word against him again, so help me God.
ALLEN. I had so much fun meeting him in the park today.
BECKY. He's ... *(With effort.)* ... a lovely man.
ALLEN. I'm jealous of him, Becky.
BECKY. You're jealous of *that* ... *(With great effort.)* ... lovely man?
ALLEN. He lives such a rich, full, productive live. He has success, money, sophistication. He's always traveling, always ... *(The doorbell rings.)* Ah, that's him! He's here! *(Stands in front of Becky.)* How do I look? How does the apartment look? Do we have Perrier? lemons? carrots? oat bran muffins? buckwheat rice cakes?
BECKY. *(Pushes back his hair; brushes off his shoulders.)* We have everything. Everything is perfect.
ALLEN. *(Moves to offstage to entrance door, L.)* Comb your hair. Color your cheeks. Puff the pillows. And don't forget to rinse out the ice-cubes! *(Sound: entrance door opening and slamming shut. Becky "puffs pillows." Offstage.)* Tommy!
TOMMY. *(Offstage.)* Al!
TOGETHER. *(Sing offstage.)*

What fun we had!
What fun we had!
We played, we danced,
We joked, we giggled,
Our behinds we wiggled ...

(Offstage laughter.)
TOMMY. *(Offstage.)* Al, this is Desiree Duchamps-Delissia Benitez, the sister of my wife.
ALLEN. *(Offstage.)* I'm very glad to meet you. *(Becky listens to all of this with a bemused expression. Allen and Tommy — without hat and briefcase — and Desiree enter. Desiree is Hispanic, shapely, white leotard, sprinkled sparsely above the waist with sequins; she wears spiked high-heeled white shoes, carries an expensive white shoulder bag with giant gold clasp; wears a broad diamond bracelet and three or four sparkling rings.)* Becky, this is Desiree Duchamps-Delissia Benitez, and my ... friend, Tommy Glenville.
TOMMY. You look wonderful, Becky. Please accept this as a

gesture of my friendship. *(He hands her a small leather box with a rose on it. Becky opens it. A bit perplexed, she holds the box out for Allen to see what's in it.)*

BECKY. It's.... It's... Ahhh.... Ohhh.... What can I say?

TOMMY. It's an ancient gold medallion of the Roman Emperor Appius Claudius.

BECKY. What can I say?

ALLEN. It's a knockout. Thank you.

BECKY. I have never in my life seen anything like it. *(Turns to Desiree.)* I'm delighted. It's charming.

ALLEN. Tommy has told me a lot about you, Desiree. *(Becky nods. She can't take her eyes off the woman.)*

DESIREE. *(Moves about impatiently; chews on gum; speaks with ghetto accent.)* He likes to talk of his Desiree. *(Snarls at Tommy.)* You are an animal. You are a delicious, savage, primitive animal. Grrr. Grrr. *(To others.)* He is extraordinary. He is the only man I met who is one-hundred percent masculine. He knows what a woman is, that is his attraction; he knows women backwards and forward, from the front and from the behind. He knows. *(Presses her backside against him.)* You have to respect a man who has such knowledge of women. I love this man so much that it takes me all of my will-power not to eat him up like a dish of chocolate-chip pistachio-peach-and-vanilla ice cream. *(Turns to face him; closely; seductively.)* Did you hear what I said, Tommy?

TOMMY. When we get home you shall live your fantasies, Desiree.

DESIREE. Whatever I want to do with you? Even if it is ugly? dirty? despicable?

TOMMY. Whatever you want, you shall have. *(Their eyes hold ferociously. Desiree growls, purrs, blows a stream of air into Tommy's face. Tommy reciprocates, purrs, growls. Their bodies are pressed together. Allen and Becky exchange wide-eyed, envious stares; what sex those two must have!)*

DESIREE. *(Moves away; laughing.)* Oh, baby, you can light my fire, any way you want! *(In Spanish; to Becky.)* He is too hot for this innocent young lady who doesn't know her ass from her elbow!

BECKY. *Si.*
TOMMY. *(To Allen.)* How do you like that?
ALLEN. She's quite a lady!
TOMMY. You think so?
ALLEN. *(Wags his hand.)* Wowee! Wowee! *(They break out in laughter, throw their arms around each other and move off, chatting happily.)*
TOMMY. I don't know what it is, but as soon as I'm with you, I fall into these laughing jags.
ALLEN. The same with me. It's incredible.
TOMMY. It's like being back in elementary school.
ALLEN. It used to happen to me all the time. The kid at the next desk would stare at me cross-eyed and I'd start laughing ... I couldn't stop ... *(A renewed burst of laughter from them; they exit. Becky hasn't taken her eyes off Desiree.)*
DESIREE. You have a gorgeous place here, Mrs. Birmingham. I love the old buildings on West End Avenue. They remind me of my childhood. *(She sits on love seat. Shortly Becky sits in armchair.)*
BECKY. Where are you from?
DESIREE. East a hundred-and-thirteenth. I used to come up to this neighborhood with my friends and steal bicycles. *(Laughs.)* Where you from?
BECKY. This neighborhood.
DESIREE. How you like that, I could have stolen your bicycle! *(Laughs.)*
BECKY. If you did, I hope you broke both your legs! *(She forces a laugh twice as loud as Desiree's.)*
DESIREE. I was a fantastic athlete when I was young. I never have an accident and nobody could every catch me.
BECKY. The royalty from Albania caught you.
DESIREE. What royalty?
BECKY. The man you married before Tommy married your sister ... *(Punches it in.)* ... Celia! Celeste! Patimkin! Lombardi!
DESIREE. Oh, him. He was no royalty. He was a check-out clerk at the A&P supermarket. And he was from Pennsylvania, not Albania. I divorced him already. And Tommy, he's in the

middle of a divorce from my sister. He was only waiting for me.

BECKY. How long do you know Tommy?

DESIREE. We have been lovers since I was fifteen. That man teaches me everything. He is a philosopher, a poet; he has a comprehension of people that is unnatural. But he is a practical man, too. He says to me one night after we have magnificent sex, he says, "Desiree, what is life? It is a game," he says. "It is many games," he says, "and what is required of us is to choose what game we want to play with our lives." He says, "For me, Desiree, the best game, the only game that is worthwhile in these modern days is the bullshit game of power." *(She rises, laughs; snaps her fingers, walks across the stage, swinging her hips, turned on by the wisdom of Tommy's words.)* "The power game!" I say to him. "Why is that, oh, wise man from the tall buildings on Wall Street?" And he says to me, "Time is short and life is shorter but money is always honey." The man knows. The man knows everything. *(She now faces audience and speaks first, out front, to musical accompaniment.)*

They make me laugh,
These rich white gringos,
These West End ladies,
Who eat too much,
And drink too much,
So they have to go,
To evening classes,
With their big fat asses,
To exercise,
And starve themselves,
For men to look at,
When there are men,
To look at,
For these West End ladies,
These rich, white gringos.

And they don't know what to do,
With their empty lives,
Nobody loves them,

Nobody gives a shit for them,
These helpless dames,
Of West End Avenue.

(And now she sings; to Becky.)

Get smart, my fancy lady,
Get wise, my lazy lady,
You don't have to beg,
For your equal rights,
For your lover's nights,
Just pick a game,
Any game,
From one to ten,
And learn to win.

Life's a game,
In these modern days,
There are many ways,
To play the game,
To win, to lose,
To pass the time,
You choose,
The choice is yours,
But when it's over,
You leave the table,
Your life, it's over.

What game you play, my fancy lady,
With the rest of your life?
Do you dig in the streets for gold?
Or become some fat creep's wife
Until you grow gray and old?
Is it sex or dope or bathtub gin?
Or the medical profession?
Or daily confession?
So you can commit another sin?
It's up to you, young lady.

(And now to audience.)

Life's a game,
In these modern days,
There are many ways,
To play the game,
To win, to lose,
To pass the time,
You choose,
The choice is yours,
But when it's over,
You leave the table,
Your life, it's over.

(She breaks into a dazzling, whirling tap dance, giving it all the show-biz pizzazz she can muster. A professional dancer/singer should be cast in role. Number ends. Becky applauds. If the audience applauds, Desiree takes a bow. Allen and Tommy enter. Allen carries a tray on which there are four tall glasses of mineral water with wedges of lime in them. Becky and Desiree move to get their drinks.)

ALLEN. Did you see that shot Walker took?

TOMMY. I was at the game.

ALLEN. You were? Really?

TOMMY. I have a row of seats behind the Knick bench. Two of them are yours for the season.

ALLEN. Great. I can go with my son.

BECKY. You really know to sing and dance. Wow, that was terrific.

DESIREE. Tommy wants me to get back into it, but I'm not interested.

BECKY. Why not? You have talent.

DESIREE. When you do it professionally, it's not so much fun. The work is hard.

BECKY. I used to daydream about taking ballet lessons. When I was in Junior High School. I was afraid to try.

(Allen, R., and Becky, L., are now seated on the love seat. Tommy is in the rocking chair; Desiree in armchair.)

TOMMY. Where are your children? I'd love to meet them.

DESIREE. What are your kids' names?

ALLEN. They're out now, but they'll be back soon.

BECKY. Zoe and Marco. Zoe is sixteen. Marco is fifteen. They'll be home for dinner.

(Becky's voice now rises clearly above the din.) Why don't you and Tommy have dinner with us?

(Sudden silence.)

ALLEN. Tommy, I'd really like that.

TOMMY. Unfortunately we have a dinner date at Lutece.

DESIREE. Let's not go. The Wellington-Tilsons are so boring. *(Silence. They all stare at Tommy, waiting for his decision.)*

TOMMY. *(Finally; a beguiling smile.)* We'll stay for dinner. *(Shouts and applause from the others.)*

BECKY. It'll be ready in fifteen minutes. *(Moves to kitchen. Desiree runs after her.)*

DESIREE. Let me help. *(Arm around each other, they move off, chatting.)*

BECKY. Does Tommy eat fish?

DESIREE. That's all he eats. He's so particular about his food. I gave up cooking for him.

BECKY. How about broccoli?

DESIREE. That's his favorite. If you put garlic on it, you'll never get rid of him. *(They exit.)*

ALLEN. It feels good having you in my home, Tommy. *(Takes off his shoes.)*

TOMMY. I already feel like family, Al. *(Takes off his shoes.)*

ALLEN. Thank you.

TOMMY. How are things at Dean and Leibnitz?

ALLEN. Fine.

TOMMY. You don't have to answer this ...

ALLEN. *(Reprimandingly; no subject is private for Tommy.)* Tommy.

TOMMY. How much do you earn there?

ALLEN. On average, a hundred-twenty thousand a year.

TOMMY. That's it?
ALLEN. Uhhh ...
TOMMY. After fourteen years?
ALLEN. Uhhh ...
TOMMY. That's not fair, Al.
ALLEN. They've been nice to me, really: vacations, health and pension, incentive bonuses ... Leibnitz treats me like his own son.
TOMMY. What do you think he earns a year.
ALLEN. Tommy, Leibnitz started the company. Thirty-five years ago. He ...
TOMMY. Two, three million a year?
ALLEN. Sure, but ...
TOMMY. *(Puts on shoes.)* Enough! You said enough! I have the picture. It makes me so damn angry when I hear something like this. Your work, your sweat, your ideas, your expertise, and he sits there, scooping the cream off the top!

(Rises; vehemently.) Damn it, Al! It's unfair! It's grossly, offensively unfair!

(Paces; murmurs.) I shouldn't have started. I should have stayed out of it. I shouldn't have opened my mouth. I should have minded my own business.

(Turns to speak to audience.) But either I'm this man's friend or I'm not. I can't play our relationship with half a heart or pretend I've acquired no insights into the uses and abuses of institutional power. Here's where I have a problem. I always have. The strong feeding off the weak. The rich manipulating the poor. Nothing has changed. Not capitalism. Not communism. Not fascism. The goal is the same for all: how do I get more at my neighbor's expense? That's it in a nutshell. Winners and losers. Take your pick. Wining is a habit. Losing is a habit. We ourselves choose, willfully and consciously, whether to be one or the other.

(Paces.) What did I have going for me when I crept into this dunghill we call life? *Nadas! Nadas!* I ate shit for breakfast, lunch and dinner; that's if I was lucky! Typical grade B story. But at an early, adolescent age, I read a book, accidentally, as it were, from motives that are wholly inexplicable to

me. I picked up a book in a local library and read it and my life changed, the course and direction of my youth was irretrievably altered. I don't, oddly enough, recall the name of the book, but it lead immediately to the reading of another and another and another. And lo and behold, hocus pocus jiminy crocus, I remade myself! I cast myself into the image of a fantasy that occurred to me one rainy windswept day in the canyons of Williamsburg, in the borough of Brooklyn. I reshaped the tone of my voice, the movement of my tongue, the precision and rhythm of my newly discovered vocabulary.

(Recites.) Draconian. Presynaptic. Onomatopoeia.

(Speaks naturally.) And I started paying particular attention to my haircuts, the length of my sideburns, the width of my shirt collars, the weight of my shoes. I conjured a posture, a walk, a manner, a physiological methodology founded on Old World class consciousness. I tore myself bodily out of the grubby roots of poverty by way of scholarship, grant, letters of recommendation and …

(Mimics young Oliver Twist.) Please, Sir, may I have the opportunity to prove my worth to you? Oh, please, Sir, may I work for endless hours, for no pay at all, to suit your fancy? Please, Sir. I'm pitifully poor and underprivileged. Please, Sir, I want *mooore.*

(Normal voice.) I hated, loathed, despised every vile moment of it. But I did what was necessary. As my predecessors had. I committed myself fully to the habit of winning, the blueprint and routine of gaining power, power which is the most fun of all, power which, I learned, is tantamount to freedom. The cry of freedom, ladies and gentlemen, is "Go fuck yourself!" in any government, in any society, at any time. Surprisingly or perhaps not surprisingly, I have come to love life, to treasure it, to accept as a given the length of its days and the silence of its eternities, and that, ladies and gentlemen, is no small accomplishment.

(Turns to Allen; forcefully.) And don't you think it's time you did something, my friend, my buddy, my comrade? How can you permit yourself to be used so shamelessly? Where is your pride, your self-respect, your competitive drive? Do you

enjoy being a loser? A pathetic hanger-on? A second-rate, nice little guy who gets a pat on the head and a couple of bucks on Christmas Eve from the big boss?

ALLEN. *(Puts on shoes, nervously.)* Tommy …

TOMMY. Will you tell me what else you have to do with your life?

ALLEN. Tommy …

TOMMY. Will you tell me what game you're playing?

ALLEN. *(Rises; a bit too loudly.)* Game? What game? I'm not playing any game!

TOMMY. Open your eyes! Look around! Don't repeat your old patterns of sloth and mediocrity.

ALLEN. *(Looks around; confused.)* So I'm looking around. I'm looking. I don't see anything. What are we talking about? *(Tommy looks around — the coast is clear. He beckons Allen to move closer to him. They stand huddled together; whisper.)*

TOMMY. You tell me.

ALLEN. *(An outburst.)* I…! *(Whispers.)* I should tell you what we're talking about?

TOMMY. What *they're* talking about.

ALLEN. *They're?* Who's *they're?*

TOMMY. Hear anything?

ALLEN. Where?

TOMMY. In the office, perhaps.

ALLEN. *(It takes all his effort to keep from exploding.)* What would I hear?

TOMMY. If you don't do something with the information, someone else will.

ALLEN. Will what? I don't…. You're confusing me! You're …

TOMMY. Acquisitions, mergers, takeovers, who's buying, selling what, where, when. Pass it on. Complete confidence. I can guarantee you half a million in additional income, per annum, free and clear. *(Allen's face loses all color. He starts breathing heavily, as if he's been running for miles.)*

ALLEN. Please…. Please, leave my home.

TOMMY. *(Shouts at once; furiously.)* Desiree! Come in here! *(Desiree rushes in, followed by Becky. Tommy jerks his head towards the entrance door and moves out. Desiree shrugs to Becky and runs after him, chatting.)*

DESIREE. What are you doing? Where we going? I'm starving, Tommy. Aren't we gonna eat today? *(Entrance door opening and slamming shut.)*

BECKY. *(After an uncomfortable beat or two.)* Allen? What happened?

ALLEN. *(Moves to sit in rocking chair.)* We had a disagreement.

BECKY. About what?

ALLEN. About ... obligations ... loyalties. *(Said with emotion.)* One.... One has to set an example, hold to a ... conviction, stand up and not be afraid to say, "I'm not like you. Life isn't a game to me. Take your games some place else. You have the wrong customer, mister."

BECKY. Is your friendship over?

ALLEN. It's over.

BECKY. Then I can tell you. He lied, Allen. He's a liar. Desiree was never married to royalty from Albania. She was married to a man who was a checkout clerk in the A&P in Pennsylvania. Anyway, she's divorced from him and Tommy's in the process of getting a divorce from her sister, and you can imagine what's going on, the cheating, the duplicity, the sickness and perversion ... *(Sticks her finger in her wide-open mouth and makes sound of throwing up. No response from Allen. Sees he's not amused.)* I'll get dinner ready. *(And she exits quickly. Allen takes off his shoes. He picks up a folded newspaper. He puts it on his lap, stares off into space. He leans back and rocks, slowly. The rocking chair creaks. Lights fade to dark.)*

END OF ACT ONE

ACT TWO

Scene 1

The King Cole Room at the St. Regis Hotel.

TIME: Several weeks later; late afternoon.

AT RISE: A rococo-style table and chairs: "stage-fake."

Tommy is seated at table, pouring champagne into two glasses. He sets the bottle in the bucket stand at his side.

On the rear screen abstract design suggesting place.

SOUND: an offstage performer singing and playing the piano: "I Can't Get Started With You," or some such lounge music.*

Allen enters, brown hat and briefcase in hand. He looks around, spots Tommy and moves to his table; he sits down.

ALLEN. I'm sorry I'm late. Thank you for coming.
TOMMY. *(Offers him glass of champagne.)* Champagne? It's a special occasion. *(Allen takes the glass from him. Tommy raises his glass. Allen hesitates: it's a decisive moment for him. He finally clicks Tommy's glasses with his own. They drink.)* How's everything?
ALLEN. Fine.
TOMMY. The children?
ALLEN. Fine.
TOMMY. Becky?
ALLEN. She's fine, too.
TOMMY. Is she?
ALLEN. Yes.

* See Special Note on Songs and Recordings on copyright page.

TOMMY. And you?
ALLEN. The same.
TOMMY. What does that mean?
ALLEN. I expect the worst. I'm a pessimist.
TOMMY. Not about Becky.
ALLEN. Yes. About Becky.
TOMMY. But it's over five years.
ALLEN. I know.
TOMMY. Statistically ...
ALLEN. She's cured. I know. But it doesn't seem to make any difference to me. I have nightmares.
TOMMY. Of what?
ALLEN. A man hanging from a tree.
TOMMY. A man?
ALLEN. Yes.
TOMMY. May I offer a suggestion?
ALLEN. I'm listening.
TOMMY. Talk to my analyst.
ALLEN. You have one?
TOMMY. For about sixteen years. That surprise you?
ALLEN. I would have thought you didn't need one. You always seem so ... comfortable with yourself.
TOMMY. I operate on the premise that we can all use whatever help we can get. Do I set up an appointment for you?
ALLEN. I'll think about it. It's weird how I can tell you things that ... *("...I can't tell anyone else," would have followed but he drops it.)* How's Desiree?
TOMMY. Ebullient. It's a secret, Al. You're the first to know. We're getting married.
ALLEN. *(Laughing.)* You're.... You and Desiree? You're.... You have to ... *("...be kidding," would have followed. The expression on Tommy's face doesn't change; he's quite serious about it. Allen twists his own features into an equally serious expression.)* Congratulations. Becky and I wish you both every happiness.
TOMMY. Why did you want to see me?
ALLEN. I ... I missed you.
TOMMY. And I you.
ALLEN. I missed ... our friendship.

TOMMY. No more than I did.
ALLEN. I've been thinking of what you asked me to do and ... I'll do it. But on one condition. I don't want a penny of your money.
TOMMY. *(Protests.)* Al ...
ALLEN. I'm serious.
TOMMY. As you wish. But you can't stop me from opening a Swiss bank account for Zoe and Marco. They'll be off to college soon.
ALLEN. How do I ... get the information to you?
TOMMY. I suggest you offer my niece, Daisy Lansing Hakim-Mustafa, employment in your office. Whatever you want to pass on to me, you give to her, on a slip of paper. I'll destroy it. You should know beforehand that my niece is disabled.
ALLEN. That doesn't ...
TOMMY. She's deaf. And mute. It's a painfully tragic story.

(Pours more champagne.) At the age of fourteen she was prima ballerina with the Lyon Ballet Company. An incredibly beautiful and talented young girl, with a brilliant career ahead of her. At the age of seventeen she married a fabulously wealthy oil sheik from the Persian Gulf, Abdul Said Hakim-Mustafa. She had everything one could desire. A year later she had a child, a lovely girl. All appeared to be idyllic. But shortly after Daisy fell madly in love with a Mexican bullfighter, Carlos Luis Ruiz Santiago, who was then living on the Costa del Sol, in Spain.

(He drinks some champagne. Allen is all ears, can't wait for him to continue.) One night she ran off with Carlos, taking the little girl with her. Going across from France to Spain, along one of those treacherous roads in the Pyrenees, their car skidded off an embankment and ... the little girl and the Mexican bullfighter were fatally injured. When Daisy's husband, Abdul Said Hakim-Mustafa, learned of this, he took his own life by jumping off the roof of the Hotel du Cap.

(Drinks a bit more.) She's been an out-patient at the Loeb Clinic since her return to the States. She still dances on occasion, but not professionally. She hasn't spoken or heard a word since the day of the accident. Her prognosis is not

encouraging.

ALLEN. I swear, I've got goose pimples all over.

TOMMY. She doesn't have to know anything about ... our arrangement.

ALLEN. No, no, definitely not.

TOMMY. If you hadn't called, I would have called you, Al. I would have apologized. I would have asked for your forgiveness. No amount of money, no accommodation, is worth our friendship. *(Allen is overwhelmed with good feelings for Tommy. He clicks Tommy's glass and they drink. Sound: Wieniawski's "Polonaise."* They rise, put on hats, pick up cases. Tommy wears gray homburg. In tempo, arm-in-arm, they cross stage, turn around, move U. and exit. Lights fade to dark.)*

Scene 2

Allen's office.

TIME: The following week: morning.

AT RISE: Allen is on the phone, putting in buy and sell orders.

On the rear screen: the market quotations; ticker tape noises.

An isolated white wooden door hangs seemingly without support, on the right, a foot or two above floor level.

SOUND: an increasing buzz of unintelligible voices behind the white door.

ALLEN. *(Into phone.)* Freddy, let me have five hundred RBCK at market; another five hundred Liz Callahan; right; what's the spread on that? No, forget it. What's the spread on Home

* See Special Note on Songs and Recordings on copyright page.

Shopping Network? Okay. Do it at the bid and sell another thousand of EM. Sell that at bid, too. Right. It's a day order.

(He becomes aware of buzzing voices behind white door; looks to door; another phone line rings; connects into it.) Hello.

(A short beat.) Sam, go ahead. Buy? Sell? Buy. Okay. How far? Five thousand? Margin? Right. Will do. You want me to put it in now or call you back? Call. Right.

(He connects back into line with Freddy; continues looking to white door; buzzing voices increase.) Freddy, it's me. Buy five thousand of Kimberly International. It's on the American. What's the spread? Okay. Take it on the offering. If you don't get it, call me back.

(He disconnects line; looks to white door; pulls a tissue from box on desk, wipes his perspiring face. Then with a great display of caution, he moves to the white door, presses his ear to it, writes on a small pad what he hears. Several words become intelligible to us: "Mycorp … takeover bid … 250 million shares … Continental … a hundred and nine … Burton Properties … ninety days … 20 percent.… Timmerman set up a meeting with Monahan … going for Chapter Eleven.… Get rid of them.… Get rid of them.… Get rid of them.… " The words reverberate, bounce off the walls, take on ominous overtones. The voices fade out. Wiping his face and hands with tissue, Allen returns to chair behind desk. There is a timid knock on the offstage entrance door. Nervously.) Yes?

(Sound: ballet music. Lights dim. Daisy enters, dancing. Spotlight on Daisy. She is wearing a tutu, white leotard, white ballet shoes, a pearl necklace. A professional ballet dancer should be cast in role. She dances beautifully, a dream come to life. The number ends with Daisy stone-still, a flower turned in on itself. Allen rises; can barely speak, so overcome is he by her loveliness.) That was.… You were.… I never …

(Daisy unfolds; smiles brightly.) Come, sit down, Daisy. Tommy told me.… About your … accident.… Your … terrible … tragedy …

(He remembers.) How dumb of me! I completely forgot …

(He shouts loudly, leaning towards her; articulates each word.) Tommy told me about your disability! Can you read my lips?

(Daisy nods. She seems to be enjoying his confusion. He moves chair for her to sit on. She sits. Pressing his face close to hers so she can read his lips.) I'll try ... to pronounce everything clearly! I am really sorry! You are a brave and courageous ...

(He shouts even more loudly for emphasis.) ... young lady!

(Tommy enters. He carries attaché case, gray homburg on head. He is all smiles.)

TOMMY. Hey, take it easy, will you? You don't have to shout. She's deaf, you idiot! *(Daisy runs to embrace him. To Daisy; speaks with slightly exaggerated articulation.)* Hi, sweetheart. Did you miss your Uncle Tommy? *(Daisy nods fervently.)*

ALLEN. *(Very nervous about Tommy being in his office.)* Tommy, do you, uhhh ... *(Whispers agitatedly; jabs finger at white door.)* Do you ... think you should be in here?

TOMMY. Relax. As a former president said during war time: you have nothing to fear but fear itself. *(Kisses Daisy on brow.)* Watch out for this man, Daisy. He's known for lusting after young girls who resemble young boys. I suggest you don't get a short haircut while in his employ.

ALLEN. *(Runs between them; sticks his face in front of Daisy.)* He.... He's joking! Your uncle's joking! *(To Tommy.)* I have ... *(Points to pad in hand.)* ... certain ... communications ... you know ... previously discussed ...

TOMMY. *(Now serious; softly.)* Follow the plan. A step at a time. Proceed. *(He moves away; whistling casually. Allen nods, drops slip of paper on the floor, with melodramatic nonchalance; moves away, whistling along with Tommy. Loudly, in case they're being listened to.)* I thought I'd drop by and take you out for the afternoon, Al. You've been working too hard. You have to learn how to play, how to enjoy the good things in life. *(In the meantime Daisy picks up slip of paper; Tommy bends to his haunches; Daisy lifts Tommy's homburg off his head, puts slip of paper on his head, replaces homburg; Tommy rises. All done to a rehearsed rhythm.)*

ALLEN. *(Loudly, to white door.)* I can't get away this afternoon. I'm sorry. I have too much to do for Mr. Leibnitz!

TOMMY. *(Shouts at white door.)* He wouldn't mind!

ALLEN. Probably not! He's a kind and generous man! But I have responsibilities here!

TOMMY. Hogwash! You're coming along, my friend. I don't know when I'll see you again. I'm going off to Europe, to buy a few paintings. There's a Kadinksy and a Giacometti that I'm particularly interested in owning. *(During above he kisses Daisy goodbye, on cheek, takes Allen's arm and leads him out of the office. Offstage door opens and slams shut. Sound: ballet music. Daisy looks about, pleased by her new surroundings; she begins dancing, joyfully, whirling around the office. No more than a minute or two: a musical button. Lights fade to dark.)*

Scene 3

On the rear screen a montage of sporting and entertainment events with appropriate sound track: the thundering finish of a horse race; an exciting play on a baseball field; a knockdown at a fight; a highlight of a frenetic basketball game; a film clip of Times Square during its peak hour; people entering theaters; guests eating and dancing in the Rainbow Room; etc.

Images on rear screen fade into an abstract design that suggest a deserted Broadway, above Ninety-sixth Street.

A "stage-fake" lamp post and old wooden newspaper stand.

SOUND: Appropriate street noises.

TIME: Several months later; after midnight.

AT RISE: Tommy is walking Allen home. They wear top hats, carry ivory-tipped evening canes.

TOMMY. *(Points with cane.)* Look at the ornament at the top of that building? You see it? No. Over there. Over there.
ALLEN. Hey, that's fantastic!
TOMMY. I suspect it's a bastardized medieval gargoyle.
ALLEN. It's the first time I saw it and I've walked home this

way hundreds of times.

TOMMY. If you notice nearly everyone walks with his eyes pasted to the pavement instead of raised to the sky. That which is beautiful is usually above us. Hence the pedestal. *(They sit on wooden newspaper stand.)*

ALLEN. I'm happy, Tommy. Right this minute I'm happy.

TOMMY. What about the man hanging from the tree?

ALLEN. He's there. He's always there. In my nightmares. In my daymares. But let's drop it, please.

TOMMY. As you wish. However, apropos of happiness ... *(Removes envelope from inside of top hat.)* There's fifty thousand dollars in cash here. No one can trace any of it. You can ...

ALLEN. *(Eyes on ground; between clenched teeth.)* Put it away! Put it away!

TOMMY. Why don't you stop ...

ALLEN. *(Looks at him.)* No! I don't want it! That's not why.... It has nothing to do with money! You don't understand anything, do you?

TOMMY. Silly. You're being perverse and silly. By the way, I'd like you to be the best man at my wedding. If you don't object. *(Replaces envelope in top hat.)*

ALLEN. *(Seduced.)* Your wedding?

TOMMY. To Desiree Duchamps-Delissia Benitez. Now I know what's going on in that head of yours, buddy: what does a high-school dropout, an ex-chorus girl, the mistress of countless sleaze-balls and dick-heads, what does she have in common with a rich, handsome, cultured, financial wizard like myself. Isn't that what you're thinking?

ALLEN. *(Can't help smiling.)* How'd you guess?

TOMMY. Omniscience. Let me enlighten you, my friend. Desiree is an extremely street-smart, astute young woman; her interests range from analytical psychology to nineteenth-century *Roman à clef* literature to pre-Columbia ceramic artifacts.

ALLEN. And she isn't a bad piece of ass either.

TOMMY. *(With broad English accent.)* I beg your pardon. How in the world would you know that?

ALLEN. *(With broad English accent.)* Oh, I have my means and methods, old chum.

TOMMY. You haven't perchance diddled my fiancee in the recent past, have you, old chap?
ALLEN. Diddled your fiancee? I can't image where you got that from.
TOMMY. From that leering, lascivious smirk on your kisser, my buggeroo buddy!
ALLEN. *Your* buggeroo buddy!
TOMMY. Yes! *My* buggeroo buddy! *(They jump off newspaper stand together, sing — without English accents — and dance, top hats on heads, canes in hand. Sound: appropriate accompaniment.)*
TOGETHER.

It's obvious we're a pair of perverts,
Hell-bent on a variety of pleasures,
Unashamedly acknowledged converts,
To a crusade for sensual treasures.

TOMMY.

It matter not,
If we pursue,
Man or woman,
Or nubile maid.

ALLEN.

And if the truth be known,
Should one be loose,
We'd be just as happy,
With a plump, fat goose!

TOMMY.

But in this age,
Of rare disease,
Transmitted by *drech* and blood,
We've been forced to abandon,
Our sinful ways.

ALLEN.

And to settle down,
With a faithful spouse,
To live the life,
Of a timorous mouse!

TOGETHER.

And yet we have to confess,

Our lives are in a mess,
Desiring as we do,
To bed every Jane and Sue.

TOMMY.

Biology has doomed us forever,
To indiscriminate lust,
There's no deceiving nature,
It's do or die or bust!

TOGETHER.

Higamous, pigamous,
Pigamous, higamous,
Woman's monogamous,
Man's polygamous,
That's how it's meant to be!
That's how it's meant to be!

Higamous, pigamous,
Pigamous, higamous,
Woman's monogamous,
Man's polygamous,
That's plain for all to see!
That's plain for all to see!

ALLEN.

If a man is randy,
And a woman is handy,
And they've had
A drink or two,
Is he to say,
I'm a married man,
I cannot give it to you?

TOMMY.

Or is he to admit,
That he is accursed,
With an unquenchable thirst,
And give her the old sc-rewww.

TOGETHER.

Higamous, pigamous,
Pigamous, higamous,

Woman's monogamous,
Man's polygamous ...

(Sound: a deep, vibrant organ chord.)

TOMMY. *(Holding on to Allen; mock fright.)*

Oh, my God,
Oh, my God,
It's time to try again!

ALLEN.

They're coming
To get you, my friend!

TOMMY.

It's time to try again!

ALLEN.

They're coming
To get you, my friend!

TOMMY.

I have to try again!

TOGETHER.

Oh, my God,
Oh, my God,
It is the veritable end!
It is the veritable end!

TOMMY.

What am I to do?
Oh, what am I to do?

ALLEN.

Marry the girl,
Take the shot,
If it doesn't gel,
Give her some dough.
And go off to Monte Carlo!
Go off to Monte Carlo!

TOMMY.

I'll do as you say,
My dear old friend,
And bind myself for life,
But should I die,
Before my wife,

Tell all of those who'll listen,
Tell all of those who'll listen:

(Whispers.)

Higamous, pigamous,
Pigamous, higamous,
Woman's monogamous,
Man's polygamous,
That's how it's meant to be!

ALLEN.

That's how it's meant to be.

TOGETHER.

Higamous, pigamous,
Pigamous, higamous,
Woman's monogamous,
Man's polygamous,
That's plain for all to see!
That's plain for all to see!

Higamous ...

(Sound: another deep, vibrant organ chord, followed by marital organ music. Lights fade and then bounce up. Formally, grimly, Allen takes Tommy by the arm, turns and leads him to a spot on stage where shafts of hazy light bring to mind a chapel. Becky leads Desiree in, to stand beside Tommy. Desiree wears a veil and a long gossamer train follows her. It is held by Daisy who is in tutu and wears a garland of flowers on her brow. Becky is wearing a wide-brimmed straw hat. Allen, Becky and Daisy step aside. It is all choreographed simply and charmingly. On rear screen, relevant design. Tommy puts a wedding ring on Desiree's finger, then lifts her veil and kisses her. Sound: applause and shouts of congratulations, a din of noise, from offstage guests. Allen, Becky and Daisy take turns hugging the newlyweds. The men hand Daisy their top hats and canes; Desiree detaches her veil and train, gives them to Daisy with her bouquet. Daisy exits. Sound: dance music; dinner is being served. On rear screen, a fading and reappearing design to catch the sense of the wedding party. Allen dances with Becky; Tommy with Desiree. Daisy returns with a tray on which there are five glasses of champagne. Everyone takes a glass. Daisy puts the tray aside.)

ALLEN. *(Raises glass; starts off a bit nervously.)* I ... I'd like to offer a toast if I may!

(Hits glass with pen to quiet the guests.) Your attention! May I have your attention, please!

(Sound: offstage chatter and music fade to silence.) But.... But before I give my toast I'd like to tell you a little story that actually happened to Tommy and me last week.

(A short beat.) After we had a delicious meal at a *nouvelle cousine* restaurant called Matagalpa on East 47th Street, we took a leisurely walk up Madison Avenue. At 59th Street, a young, disabled, black shoeshine boy asked us if we'd like a shoeshine. Without thinking twice, Tommy said to him, "Follow me, please." I had no idea what Tommy was going to do, nor did the young, disabled, black shoeshine boy, but we both followed Tommy up 59th Street and into the Plaza Hotel. At the reception desk, Tommy asked the young, disabled, black, shoeshine boy what his name was. "Albert," came the reply. Tommy turned to the receptionist and said, "I want the honeymoon suite. Mr. Albert will be staying for the weekend." And with that he put his business card on the counter and walked out of the hotel, not even waiting for the young, disabled, black, shoeshine boy to say, "Thank you."

(Sound: enthusiastic applause from offstage guests. Tommy acknowledges the response by raising his glass and bowing.) Since I've known Tommy Glenville, I've come to feel towards him as I would ... a brother. Never having had a brother, you can imagine how much that means to me.

(It takes all his effort to keep from bawling.) Tommy is a man of great sophistication ... sensitivity ... and he has, as everybody knows, a devasting sense of humor.

TOMMY. *(Bowing.)* I have nothing further to say, ladies and gentlemen. *(Chuckles from offstage guests.)*

ALLEN. Born in the ghettos of Williamsburg, Brooklyn, the offspring of an impoverished fur salesman, he was raised with holes in his pockets and even bigger holes in his shoes.

TOMMY. *(Lifts foot to examine sole of shoe.)* Yeup, the holes are still there. *(Laughter from offstage guests.)*

ALLEN. But by dint of his own efforts he rose to preeminence in the financial world. And yet, there are people today who have been casting aspersions against this man's character. I am referring specifically to an article last week in you-know-what magazine and an equally scurrilous article yesterday in you-know-what newspaper.

(Hisses and murmurs of disapproval from offstage guests.)

Tommy Glenville remains an example to all of us, a symbol, a paradigm, and whenever we despair of our own lives, or the economic course pursued by our beloved country, *vis à vis,* Japan and Germany, we can look to him for inspiration and encouragement, and say in the words of the immortal bard, Walt Whitman:

(Builds emotionally.)

"Here, take this gift,
I was reserving it for some hero, speaker, or general,
One who should serve the good old cause, the great
idea, the progress and freedom of the race,
Some brave confronter of despots, some daring rebel;
But I see that what I was reserving belongs to you..."

My friend.... My brother ... Tommy Glenville! *(He throws his arms out, runs to embrace Tommy, filled with affection for the man. Tommy pats him on the back, appreciatively. Shouts and applause from offstage guests. Sound: dance music. On the rear screen, a swirl of colors. Allen takes a handkerchief from Daisy, wipes his perspiring face, and moves off to the side with her, chatting inaudibly, Desiree turns to Becky.)*

DESIREE. *(Staring at Allen and Daisy as she whispers.)* There is your trouble. She is a vampire when it comes to men. She sucks their blood like other women drink Hojo orange juice for breakfast. You will not hear me mention her name to you again. *(She moves to Tommy. Becky turns to stare at Allen who is now dancing, closely, with Daisy. Lights fade to dark.)*

Scene 4

Lights up on Daisy's apartment: a white wooden table and two white wooden chairs; a white side table, with a white telephone on it.

On rear screen, appropriate design suggesting a bright, expensive apartment.

TIME: Several weeks later; late afternoon.

AT RISE: Allen and Daisy enter, both wearing hats and carrying brown paper bags filled with groceries. Allen's briefcase is tucked under his arm.

He speaks exaggeratedly, with his face in front of Daisy so she can read his lips — he has to run about to stand in front of her.

ALLEN. *(More hyper than usual: there's trouble on the horizon.)* I enjoy shopping. I really enjoy it. Becky is the exact opposite. She hates it. She'll do anything other than go shopping. But I can go shopping at the drop of a hat. All you have to say is let's go shopping and I'm ready to go, I'm out the door, the money is jiggling in my pockets. I don't know what it is but I have always loved to go shopping!

(He places grocery bags, briefcase and hat on side table.) Do you mind if I use your phone?

(Daisy shakes her head; removes her hat.) Thank you.

(Daisy moves into offstage kitchen with grocery bags. Allen makes certain she's left before picking up phone and tapping out number. He whispers into phone.) Becky? Hi. How's it going? The kids? God. Becky, did I … get any calls?

(A short beat.) Mr. Leibnitz twice, Tommy three times…. No one else? I know. I know. I've been out all afternoon. Look, if I get any more calls, tell them you don't know where

I am or when I'm getting home. You have no idea. No, no, everything's fine. Nothing's wrong. I said nothing.

(Hangs up; thinks a beat, head bowed. Daisy enters, moves to side table, lifts grocery bags and starts for kitchen.) Can I help you? Do you want me to do anything?

(Daisy shakes her head.) This is a great place. I don't know how you can afford it, unless Tommy's giving you extra money or you've inherited ...

(He stops her from moving into kitchen, takes grocery bags from her, places them on white table; then holds her arms, stares at her.) Daisy.... Everything's beginning to get ... complicated. I've never been so confused ... about so much.... You're beautiful. I feel dizzy looking at you, as if I'm gonna faint any second. You are so beautiful ... I ... I have to ... *(He moves to kiss her, running his hands over her breasts, but she holds him back, smiles, gestures for him to be patient; she pecks at his lips. Then she grabs the grocery bags and moves toward kitchen. In her rush one of the bags or something in it falls to the floor.)*

DAISY. Son-of-a-bitch! There are eggs...!

(Spontaneously uttered in a surprisingly adolescent voice; resolved, she puts grocery bags back on white table.) I ... I have a big mouth. My parents always accused me of that. This has been without exception the worst day of my life.

(Sits at table, L.) I could feel the tension in the office, all day, all week. You hiding and everybody trying to find you. It's turning into a first-class disaster for you and Tommy, isn't it?

(No response from Allen. His face is ashen. His stare forces her to look at him.) I told Tommy I didn't know if I could do it. People keep forgetting how young I am. He said he wanted somebody in the office he could trust. But who knows what the real story is with him.

(A short beat.) I'm a student at Juilliard. He promised me a job next season with the Lyon Ballet Company if I went along.

ALLEN. What about your personal tragedies?

DAISY. What personal tragedies?

ALLEN. The Mexican bullfighter, your daughter, the car

accident ...

DAISY. I don't have a daughter. You have to be joking. And where would I find a Mexican bullfighter? Jesus Christ, who told you this utterly bizarre story.

ALLEN. Your uncle.

DAISY. My uncle?

ALLEN. Tommy.

DAISY. Don't make me laugh. I'll get nauseous. Tommy isn't my uncle. He.... He's my boyfriend. *(Sudden outburst.)* Desiree knows all about it! Everybody knows all about it so it's no big secret!

ALLEN. It's a secret to me! I didn't know *all* about it! I owe you and Tommy a tremendous vote of thanks. You certainly taught me a lesson! Too bad I have to pay such a heavy price for it!

DAISY. Who told you to listen to him? You didn't have to get involved!

ALLEN. Is that your excuse for lying to me?

DAISY. Let's not argue, huh? I consider you my friend, Allen. I'd like us to continue to be ... friends.

ALLEN. Sure. Friends. You and Tommy should have a long talk about what the hell a friend is!

DAISY. *(A short beat.)* I'm going away. I already made arrangements. It's over between Tommy and me. I thought, from the way you acted, from the way you stared at me all the time.... You wouldn't be interested in coming with me, would you?

(Allen gets his hat and briefcase.) Allen?

(He turns to her.) If I didn't accidentally ... talk before ... everything would have been different between us, wouldn't it?

(Allen stares at her for a beat, without answering.) Wouldn't it, Allen? Wouldn't it?

(Sound: ballet music. Allen puts on his hat, exits, decisively.) Wouldn't it? Wouldn't it?

(Daisy leans against the table and does a graceful stretching exercise or two. Lights fade to dark.)

Scene 5

Lights up on the Birmingham living room.

TIME: Same day; a while later.

AT RISE: On the rear screen, appropriate design.

Becky is seated in armchair, feet up on hassock. She is reading the last sentence of Jane Austen's Pride and Prejudice, *aloud.*

BECKY. "With the Gardners, they were always on the most intimate terms. Darcy, as well as Elizabeth, really loved them; and they were both ever sensible of the warmest gratitude towards the persons who, by bringing her to Derbyshire, had been the means of uniting them."

(She closes the book, ooohs and aahs with vicarious pleasure. At once she picks up Mansfield Park *and starts reading aloud.)* "About thirty years ago, Miss Maria Ward, of Huntingdon, with only seven thousand pounds, had the good luck to captivate Sir Thomas Bertram, of Mansfield Park, in the country of Northampton, and to be thereby raised to the rank of a baronet's lady, with all the comforts and consequences of a handsome house and large income. All Huntingdon exclaimed on the greatness of the match..."

(Sound: entrance door opening and slamming shut. Becky puts down book.) Allen?

ALLEN. *(Offstage.)* I'm home, dear! How did your day go? Anything out of the ordinary happen during my absence? Where are the kids? Are they in trouble? Did they get expelled from school? Is Zoe pregnant? Is Marco experimenting with drugs?

BECKY. They're in their bedrooms, studying. They've been angels all day. They're lovely children, Allen. Everyone says so. I'm not the only one.

ALLEN. *(Enters, carrying an armful of gift-wrapped packages.)* We have to stay on top of them. We have to exercise control and discipline. You don't know the young people nowadays, Becky. They're not like we were at their age. Instant gratification is their guiding principle. *(He presses the packages on her.)*

BECKY. What is all this?

ALLEN. I was saving them for you, for Christmas, for Mother's Day, for your birthday, but I want you to have them now. *(She starts opening packages. He paces agitatedly.)* Why do we put off for tomorrow what we can do today? What's wrong with us? We're letting life slip us by; we're growing old without accumulating enough memories, adventures, events, to look back on, to reflect on, to remember with thanksgiving when there's nothing laying ahead of us. We have to ...

BECKY. *(Holds up blouse.)* This is lovely, Allen. It's what I've been meaning to buy for myself for so long. It's ... *(Puts it aside; opens another package.)* Oh, Tommy called four times already and Mr. Leibnitz called three times. They want you to return their ...

ALLEN. *(Still pacing.)* Don't get me off the subject. Don't bring Tommy and Leibnitz into this. I had my fill of those two for one day. *(Turns to her.)* Guess where I was before I came home?

BECKY. With Daisy.

ALLEN. *(With dismay.)* How did you guess?

BECKY. I put two and two together. *(Their eyes hold for a painful beat.)*

ALLEN. Don't you ... like the presents I bought you?

BECKY. *(With effort.)* Yes.... Yes. I do. I do. They're all ... lovely.

ALLEN. *(Sits in rocking chair; takes off shoes.)* Anyway, I went shopping with Daisy. I spent a little time with her. I had the opportunity to see things from another perspective, another point of view. And as I was walking home, I said to myself ... *(The phone rings. They both turn to phone. Upset, Allen turns away from phone, continues.)* I said to myself ... I said.... We ... you and me.... We have a ... a great marriage, a ... a terrific marriage, especially when you take into account how many couples are getting divorced, separating, breaking, splitting ... *(The phone ringing makes it impossible for him to go on.)*

BECKY. Do you want me to answer? It could be Tommy or ...

ALLEN. No!

BECKY. What did you do? Will you tell me what you did?

ALLEN. There's nothing to tell! Nothing happened! I helped out a friend, that's all, that...! *(The phone stops ringing.)* Where was I? What was I.... *(Puts on shoes; rises; paces.)* Couples divorcing, that's it, couples divorcing and separating and ... and.... Not me. Not us. That's the point I'm making. Our marriage ... *(Senses that Becky is retreating inside herself.)* Becky? *(No response. Shouts in panic.)* Becky!

BECKY. Yes, Yes, I heard you. Our marriage ...

ALLEN. Right! That's what I was saying. Our marriage is as solid as a rock. Seventeen years. It's an achievement, an accomplishment. We should be proud of it, acknowledge it, say it, frequently. Our marriage is of immeasurable value, priceless, unique, one of a kind. We shouldn't let that fact disappear into thin air. We should write it down on a piece of paper; we should find a way to put it in concrete, in lead, in gold, so that we can hold onto it, in our hands, read it, say it aloud, every day, every hour, every ... *(Stares at her, apprehensively; softly.)* Becky. *(No response.)* Don't do it to me. Don't. Please, don't.

BECKY. Don't do what?

ALLEN. Go away from me.

BECKY. *(Rises.)* I'm not! I'm not! Allen, I can't believe how lucky I am. My life has exceeded my expectations. If you hadn't come along, if we hadn't met, married, raised a family, lived a life together, happily, happily.... Oh, there was a rough patch here and there, a period of adjustment, differing opinions ... lapses ... but in the main, generally, overall, happily, oh, so, so happily.... If not for you ... *(Stops talking, sniffs at air. Allen also starts sniffing.)*

ALLEN. What.... What's that?

BECKY. It smells like something's burning.

ALLEN. Is there anything on the gas range?

BECKY. No, What could it be?

ALLEN. *(The light dawns.)* Aha! Aha! *(Shouts.)* Marco! Zoe!

Come in here! *(To Becky.)* One of them is smoking pot.

BECKY. *(Hands to face.)* Oh, nooo.

ALLEN. I want the both of you in here! This minute!

BECKY. *(Shouts.)* How could you do this to us? How? *(The phone rings. Filled with dread, Allen and Becky look to phone, again and again, afraid to pick it up.)*

ALLEN. I want you kids to understand one thing once and for all!

BECKY. Listen to your father!

ALLEN. There are guidelines in this house! There are standards of behavior!

BECKY. That man has given you every advantage!

ALLEN. So long as you are under this roof, you will abide by the rules your mother and I have set down for you!

BECKY. Answer your father! He's talking to you!

ALLEN. *(He can't take his eyes off the phone; anguished.)* There is a right and there is a ... a wrong! There is socially acceptable behavior and ... and there is socially ... unacceptable.... We live in a world.... We have to choose, take a position, conviction, belief, stand up and not be afraid to ... to say, I'm not ... like you! Life isn't a game and ... and when I speak, I ... I demand! I insist! As your ... father! I will not tolerate from my children.... Under no ... circum ... circumstances ... no, not as long as I ... not ... as long as ... I ...

(He can't go on. The phone continues to ring. Finally Allen picks it up. Into phone; softly.) Yes.

(A short beat.) I've been busy. Can't it ...

(Resigned.) I'll leave now.

(Hangs up; to Becky.) I'm ashamed of myself. I always thought I had ... ideas. To hold onto. To fight with. But when I reached inside to grab them ... I found that there was nothing in there. Nothing inside me. Nothing. But ... cobwebs.

(A short beat.) I'm sorry. I am ... sorry.

(He turns and exits. Becky covers her face and sobs quietly. Offstage we hear entrance door opening and slamming shut. Lights fade to dark.)

Scene 6

Area in Central Park. Same as Act One, Scene 2.

Tommy is seated on bench, leg crossed, no hat, no attaché case.

On rear screen, appropriate design.

TIME: Early evening.

AT RISE: Allen enters, breathlessly; no hat, no briefcase.

As soon as he enters, he sees Tommy. He walks slowly to the bench. He sits beside Tommy.

SOUND: "Polonaise," faintly; fades out.*

Tommy uncrosses leg; crosses the opposite leg; he looks to Allen.

Allen doesn't cross his leg at all.

TOMMY. I'm being investigated by the S.E.C. *(No response from Allen.)* They'll be asking you questions. Have they been in touch with you?
ALLEN. *(Stares straight ahead.)* With Leibnitz. He called to see me this afternoon. His voice sounded peculiar. I left the office early, without seeing him.
TOMMY. It's not as bad as it appears, old chum. *(Gives up frivolous tone.)* If we play our cards right, the consequences could be minimal. I need time to negotiate. I'm depending on you to give me that time.
ALLEN. And how would I do that?

* See Special Note on Songs and Recordings on copyright page.

TOMMY. Take the heat off me for a while. Tell them you approached me with inside information. I'll claim I was unaware it was inside information and that I was duped …

ALLEN. Just what kind of idiot do you take me for?

TOMMY. Al, there isn't time …

ALLEN. Now there isn't time! But you had plenty of time to lie to me and fill me with those bullshit stories about Melissa nee Upjohn Cartwright and Celia Celeste Patimkin Lombardi and your mistress, Daisy Lansing Hakim-Mustafa or whatever the hell her real name is, didn't you?

TOMMY. I don't lie, Allen.

ALLEN. *(Mimics him.)* Oh, I don't lie, Allen! I'm not a liar, not me, Allen! *(Normal voice.)* That's news to me, buddy! So far as I'm concerned you lied to me from the first day we met!

TOMMY. Not true. I'll grant you that on occasion I'm guilty of dramatizing events, for the sake of a more interesting conversation. It's a harmless practice that I don't indulge in when it comes to anything of importance.

ALLEN. If I believed that, I'd believe in the tooth fairy. *(Rises; paces.)* What an idiot I was, listening to you, getting myself into this mess. *(Turns to Tommy.)* You know what you are? You're an intellectual fascist, that's what you are! You don't give a shit for anybody but yourself!

TOMMY. What I'm suggesting, Allen, can turn a losing game into a winning one for you.

ALLEN. Do me a favor. Stop playing games with me. When I first met you I had a degree of self-respect. Now I can't even look my kids in the face. You are something. You are really something. All you want me to do is tell them you had no idea I was giving you inside information. It was all my fault.

TOMMY. For starters, yes.

ALLEN. For starters. Terrific. And they'll send *me* to jail if I tell them that, won't they?

TOMMY. They'll send you to jail no matter what you tell them, Allen. If you take my advice, however, you'll get out within a reasonably brief period of time.

ALLEN. You'll guarantee it.

TOMMY. Yes.

ALLEN. Nothing can go wrong. It's fool proof.

TOMMY. Yes. I've discussed it with my attorneys at length. While negotiating a settlement with the S.E.C., I'll make demands on your behalf. Should you go to trial, my attorneys will represent you; at my expense, of course.

ALLEN. Of course. I don't know why I'm so pig-headed. All I have to do is trust you; believe what you're telling me. Why do I have so much trouble with that, buddy?

TOMMY. I opened two Swiss bank accounts in Zoe and Marco's names, sixty thousand dollars each.

ALLEN. I told you not to! I specifically said ... I didn't want a penny from you, not a penny! Why is that so hard for you to understand?

TOMMY. I did it months ago, Allen. Foolishly as it turns out. I also donated two-hundred-and-fifty-thousand dollars to the oncology department at Lenox Hill Hospital. If for any reason, God forbid, Becky has to avail herself of their facilities.... She'll be given the very best care and attention, the very best that love and money can buy. *(Allen is visibly affected by Tommy's gesture.)*

ALLEN. Is that true?

TOMMY. Yes. I beg you to trust me this one more time. Please. Trust me. *(Allen stares at him a beat, then turns and exits, U.R. Tommy watches him leave. He then faces front, looks out at audience, expressionally. Sound: "Polonaise,"* faintly. Slowly, Tommy crosses his leg. Lights fade to dark.)*

Scene 7

Lights up on prison visitors' room.

TIME: Some months later: day.

AT RISE: SOUND: cell doors opening and slamming shut.

* See Special Note on Songs and Recordings on copyright page.

Allen is seated on a brown wooden chair that faces an empty chair on the other side of a rectangular brown wooden table. His head is resting on his arm which lies on the table.

On the rear screen, an appropriate design.

Tommy enters, stands silently for a few beats, watching Allen, before sitting in the empty chair. He puts his hat and attaché case on the table.

TOMMY. Allen?

(Startled, Allen sits upright.) I apologize for not coming to see you sooner. My attorneys forbid me. When I heard you were sentenced to a year in prison, I ... I hated myself, and I was too embarrassed to write or ...

(Allen pushes his chair away from table, angles it to face front.) We reached a settlement with the S.E.C. late yesterday. I've been fined a substantial amount of money and the likelihood is that I'll also be spending a little time in here.

(Grins.) How's the food?

(No response from Allen.) Bad joke. I've agreed to tell them everything I know, name names and all that nonsense. On balance we did extremely well, buddy. The financial community offers hope and compassion to its prodigal sons. I've already been approached with several opportunities for investment that seem very promising. In many respects I'm much better off today than I was when this whole hullabaloo started.

(Leans toward him; confidentially.) Al, I'd like to set aside something for you. There's no need for you to worry about the future. You'll be guaranteed ...

(Giving it up; angles his chair to face front; loudly.) All right, all right! We don't have to go into it now. Just keep it in mind.

ALLEN. *(Without looking at him.)* Is that all you have to say to me?

TOMMY. Not quite. Tomorrow morning I present myself before the Honorable Judge Elkins. In the opinion of my attorneys, you'll be out of here within the week.

ALLEN. *(Turns to him.)* How?
TOMMY. Your sentence will be reduced to time already served. That was one of the conditions of my pleading guilty to a single felony count.
ALLEN. You're ... positive...?
TOMMY. I'm positive.
ALLEN. I'll be out of here ...
TOMMY. Within the week. I'm disappointed, buddy. Why are you so surprised that I'm a man of his word?
ALLEN. I ... I wasn't ...
TOMMY. I don't lie, Al.
ALLEN. *(A splinter of a smile.)* You dramatize events.
TOMMY. A self-indulgence.
ALLEN. May I ask you a question?
TOMMY. Please.
ALLEN. When you say I'll be out within the week, is that dramatizing events or is that a statement of fact?
TOMMY. As I told you, in matters of importance, I don't dramatize.
ALLEN. It's a statement of fact.
TOMMY. That's right.
ALLEN. *(Grabs his hand.)* Thank you, Tommy. Thank you.
TOMMY. What you did for me no one has ever done before: you put yourself on the line and asked nothing in return.
ALLEN. Because ...
TOMMY. What?
ALLEN. Can't you guess?
TOMMY. I'd like to hear *you* say it.
ALLEN. We're friends.
TOMMY. Good, close, intimate friends.
ALLEN. Yes.
TOMMY. Ultimately we don't know why.
ALLEN. We don't.
TOMMY. Chemistry. Sociology. Race. There are attributes of the human psyche that can't be explained. *(He crosses his leg.)*
ALLEN. They can't be explained. *(He crosses his leg.)*
TOMMY. Can I confide in you?
ALLEN. If not me, who?

TOMMY. I've started taking private lessons with Father McKinney at St. Patrick's.

ALLEN. You're not going to...?

TOMMY. The odds are I will.

ALLEN. Nooo.

TOMMY. Yeup. Within a few months I'd say.

ALLEN. I never thought of you as someone who would need to ...

TOMMY. "Vanity of vanities, all is vanity. What profit has a man from all his labors under the sun? One generation goes, and another generation comes; but the earth abides forever." We have to take whatever help we can get, my friend.

ALLEN. It's not another game for you, is it?

TOMMY. Of course it's another game. That's all there is. But it may very well be the only game worth playing, the game with the highest stakes.

ALLEN. *(Shakes his head.)* I couldn't ...

TOMMY. I offer you this thought, Allen, in partial return: don't treat life too seriously. Nothing out there does.

ALLEN. I'll think about it. I will. *(Rises.)* It's amazing, our relationship, isn't it?

TOMMY. It is amazing. *(Rises.)* The times we had together ...

ALLEN. The things we've been through ...

TOMMY. Do you remember the night we met at John Dooley's cocktail party?

ALLEN. Do I? *(And they start singing and stomping their shoes, facing front.)*

TOGETHER.

What fun we had!
What fun we had!

TOMMY.

People stopped to stare at us!

ALLEN.

They couldn't believe what happened to us!

TOMMY.

We carried on like two old buddies!

ALLEN.

On their vacation without any worries!

TOGETHER.

Having fun!
Having fun!
Having ... Having ... Having ...
Having ... Having ... Having ...

(They break out in laughter. Almost at once Tommy's expression changes to a solemn one.)

TOMMY. Al? *(A short beat.)* Thank you. *(Allen nods, solemnly.)* This doesn't come easy for one of my disposition, but ... I love you, buddy. I always will. *(He puts out his hand. Allen takes it. Their eyes hold. Tommy turns abruptly to exit, R. Becky enters, wearing hat, carrying pocketbook and gloves. Tommy throws her a kiss, exits, hat on head, attaché case in hand. Becky watches him leave, then moves to Allen.)*

BECKY. Allen! *(They embrace.)*

ALLEN. He's testifying tomorrow. They made a deal. I'll be out within the week.

BECKY. We're so lucky! We are so lucky!

ALLEN. *(Moves away.)* He really was something, hon. I mean, he actually said he loved me, he used those exact words, and he said, he begged me, to take money from him. I wouldn't, but just the same.... What I did was dumb. I'm not excusing my own stupidity, but.... He didn't lie to me. He came through when it counted. He kept his part of the bargain.

BECKY. He did. No question about it.

ALLEN. If I wanted to take his money, I wouldn't have to worry for the rest of my life.

BECKY. I'm glad you didn't.

ALLEN. But he offered it to me, that's the point.

BECKY. He's ... *(With effort.)* ... generous.

ALLEN. He is generous. We're both generous when it comes to protecting one another.

BECKY. You're family.

ALLEN. We are family. No doubt about that. *(Sits at table; brightly.)* So. How are the kids? Did anybody call? Did I get any mail? There must be plenty of talk going on. What do the kids say when they think you're not listening?

BECKY. *(Sits at table; tries to suppress her anxiety.)* They're very,

very proud of you, Allen. They know you're here because you wouldn't betray a friend. Zoe said, "Tell Dad I love him and I can't wait until he gets home so I can make buttermilk pancakes for him." And Marco came up to me before I left today and he said, "Tell Dad I was the one who smoked the pot that day in my room. It wasn't Zoe. Tell him I did it because of peer pressure but I learned my lesson and I'll never do it again."

ALLEN. I let them down, Becky.

BECKY. No. No.

ALLEN. I didn't give them enough guidance, enough support, enough ...

BECKY. No. I told you. They're proud. They understand. They look up to you. We've been blessed, Allen. We have been blessed. We mustn't forget that ... even though ... regardless ... in spite of ... *(A sigh escapes from her.)* I saw Doctor Leonard last week.

ALLEN. *Last* week?

BECKY. I didn't want to ... *("Bother you" would have followed.)*

ALLEN. That's not what we agreed. We agreed you'd tell me, immediately. You promised.... You swore ...

BECKY. I know. I know. It won't happen again, I promise, I swear ... *(Cheerfully.)* Doctor Leonard said everything's fine, it is, everything's ... *(Suddenly grim.)* It came back. The same place. That's the bad news. *(Forces a big smile.)* The good news is that Doctor Leonard says it's *in situ;* that means it's localized, it hasn't spread, he says, he believes, it's an aberration, an oddity, and now all he has to do is remove it and in his judgment, in his opinion, he says, he believes, that should be no problem, and soon we'll all be together, the entire family, and we'll all ...

ALLEN. *(Numbly.)* When does he...?

BECKY. Tomorrow morning.

ALLEN. *(Without any discernible emotion.)* Did he say how long you'll be in the hospital?

BECKY. Three days. He was very emphatic about that. Three days.

ALLEN. I'll call Tommy's lawyer. I have to be there. But my

instinctual response, my ... initial reaction ... I'm convinced from what you said that there's no danger.

BECKY. There isn't. I know there isn't. Doctor Leonard never speaks glibly or loosely or imprecisely. If he didn't think, believe, that in his opinion, it was localized, *in situ,* he wouldn't have said it, period. I have to add.... He did intimate, kind of suggest, explain in some detail, that until he goes in there and sees for himself ...

ALLEN. Don't speculate.

BECKY. I'm not.

ALLEN. Don't fantasize.

BECKY. I won't.

ALLEN. Did he in any shape, manner or form mention the word.... Did he say.... Did he ... bring up.... Did he refer to ... *(He can't say it.)*

BECKY. Metastasize?

ALLEN. *(Nods.)* Yes.

BECKY. He did not.

ALLEN. But he did when we first went to him, when he first saw and he first diagnosed ... originally ...

BECKY. Yes, he did. He spelled everything out. He brought up everything that could conceivably happen. He held nothing back from us. He must have said the word metastasize at least twenty times.

ALLEN. There's your clue.

BECKY. It is a clue.

ALLEN. This time he didn't mention that ... that word once, not once. I'm convinced there's no danger. *(A buzzer sounds signifying that visiting is over. Allen and Becky rise.)*

BECKY. *(Means what she says.)* I know. I'm not worried. I trust Doctor Leonard. I'll be out of the hospital in three days and we'll all be together.

ALLEN. *(Voice filled with emotion.)* You've changed so much these past few years.... It's amazing. I can't get over it. Your whole face.... It glows with such a fantastic light.... You're.... You're the ... only woman ... I have ever loved in my life.

BECKY. *(Quickly, with embarrassment.)* Thank you. Thank you. Thank you. Thank you. Thank you. *(She hugs him; kisses him on cheek; breaks away.)* I'm happy. I'm very, *very* happy. *(She turns and exits.)*

ALLEN. *(Softly.)* Becky?

(A bit louder but not loud; a cry, "Don't go away from me!") Becky!

(Allen turns to speak to the audience. On rear screen, in silhouette, a black-and-white photograph of a man hanging from the limb of a tree appears. Sound: blade dropping on guillotine. And with a guillotine-like sound for each, four, five or more screens, all at different angles, drop: on each screen there's a silhouette of a man hanging from the limb of a tree. Gradually the photographs fade from the screens and are replaced by a bright, glaring electric-white luminosity.) She's optimistic. I have trouble with optimists. They make me uncomfortable. Personally I always expect the worst.

(A short beat.) It's a curse. Having an imagination is a curse.

(A short beat.) But.... You know what amazes me? Really amazes me? It's that she, my wife, can convince herself, emotionally and mentally convince herself, that everything's going to be all right; fine, just fine. She has confidence in her doctor; she accepts what the hospital tells her; she doesn't question the accuracy of the lab reports. It's all sci-en-ti-fic for her, all above board, all neat and predictable. Well, let me ask you this: how ... how naive can a person be? What prevents her from recognizing the dangers, the consequences of what they're talking about? *They do not know,* the doctor said; *they do not know until they get in there and they look and they see! They do not know until then! Until that second in time, what they'll find!* So how the hell can she be so damn sure about anything? You saw her! You saw how she acted! Where the hell does all that come from? Where does she get it from? Where? Where?

(Paces; kneads hands.) Well.... Well.... Maybe.... Maybe.... And I've thought about this. Plenty of times. Maybe.... Somehow.... She's managed to turn the tables on me, switch things around a little. Of course she doesn't have to worry! She's free and clear! It's *my* body that ... that's somehow infected, that ... that's filled with ... that ... that has ... it. Not hers! Not hers! Don't ask me how she did it but she

did it! She managed it! The result is, the consequences are, she's fine; she's just fine. It's my problem now. It's something I have to deal with. It's me hanging from that tree, not her, not her or anybody else, that's the simple, basic truth of it!

(A short beat.) I swear, if I get through this ... if I'm ... lucky this one more time ... and ... and it's only there, *in situ,* local, contained, and nothing has ... spread, moved, traveled, deeper, wider, elsewhere ... I swear, my plan, my intention, my resolve, is to see if I can find some ... enterprise, endeavor, effort ... that'll drain from me all my excessive ... anxieties and ... and apprehensions and ... and nightmares.

(Stands in place; faces front.) A game. What I have to do now ... is find a game. To play. To be involved in. To get lost in. A game. Any game. A game of God, of spiritual, of theology, meditation, transcendentalism, mysticism or ... or a game of ... of power, position, status, money, wealth, riches, success, business, entrepreneur, arbitrage, career, self-improvement, physical fitness, diet, health classes, exercise, aerobics, dance, volleyball, tennis, running or ... or analysis, creativity, finger-painting, song-writing, ceramic tiles, cookie jars, chess, checkers, movies, television, theater, opera, participate in a variety of ... activities ... of ... of ... or ... social services, community, family, institutions, country, nuclear, political, racial or ... or ... or ... something, anything, with passion, commitment, dedication, fun, joy, abandonment or ... or ... or ... or ... or ... or ...

(A short beat.) A game. I have to ... find ... a game. To play. Like.... Like my friend, Tommy Glenville. *(He stares out at the audience, seemingly looks into every face in the theater. Sound: "Polonaise in D."* Lights draw in to a bright spot on Allen's face. Fade to dark.)*

* See Special Note on Songs and Recordings on copyright page.

PROPERTY LIST

Felt hat (ALLEN)
Briefcase (ALLEN)
Homburg hat (TOMMY)
Cream-colored attaché case (TOMMY)
Calendar wristwatch (TOMMY)
Wristwatch (ALLEN)
N.Y. *Times* newspaper (BECKY)
Newspapers and magazines (BECKY)
Bouquet of flowers (ALLEN)
Flower vase (BECKY)
Small leather box with a rose on top containing an ancient gold medallion (TOMMY)
Tray with 4 tall glasses of water with lime wedges (ALLEN)
Champagne bucket stand (TOMMY)
Bottle of champagne (TOMMY)
2 glasses for champagne (TOMMY)
Box of tissues (ALLEN)
Slip of paper (ALLEN)
Top hats (TOMMY, ALLEN)
Ivory tipped evening canes (TOMMY, ALLEN)
Envelope with money (TOMMY)
Wedding ring (TOMMY)
Wedding veil and train (DESIREE)
Wedding bouquet (DESIREE)
Tray with 5 glasses of champagne (DAISY)
Pen (ALLEN)
Handkerchief (DAISY)
Brown paper bags with groceries (ALLEN, DAISY)
Hat (DAISY)
Books, *Pride & Prejudice* and *Mansfield Park* (BECKY)
Gift-wrapped packages (ALLEN)
  one with woman's blouse
Hat (BECKY)
Pocketbook (BECKY)
Gloves (BECKY)

SOUND EFFECTS

Clicking of old-time ticker tape
Clanging of stock market bell
Bedroom door opening and slamming shut
Front door opening and slamming shut
Doorbell
Increasing buzz of unintelligible voices
Thundering finish of a horse race
An exciting play on a baseball field
Knockdown at a fight
Highlight of frenetic basketball game
Street noises
Organ sound
Applause and shouts of congratulations
Party sounds
Dance music
Applause
Hisses
Shouts and applause
Phone ringing
Prison cell doors opening and slamming shut
Prison buzzer
Blade dropping on guillotine

TODAY'S HOTTEST NEW PLAYS

❑ **MOLLY SWEENEY by Brian Friel, Tony Award-Winning Author of *Dancing at Lughnasa*.** Told in the form of monologues by three related characters, *Molly Sweeney* is mellifluous, Irish storytelling at its dramatic best. Blind since birth, Molly recounts the effects of an eye operation that was intended to restore her sight but which has unexpected and tragic consequences. *"Brian Friel has been recognized as Ireland's greatest living playwright. Molly Sweeney confirms that Mr. Friel still writes like a dream. Rich with rapturous poetry and the music of rising and falling emotions...Rarely has Mr. Friel written with such intoxicating specificity about scents, colors and contours." - New York Times.* [2M, 1W]

❑ **SWINGING ON A STAR (The Johnny Burke Musical) by Michael Leeds. 1996 Tony Award Nominee for Best Musical.** The fabulous songs of Johnny Burke are perfectly represented here in a series of scenes jumping from a 1920s Chicago speakeasy to a World War II USO Show and on through the romantic high jinks of the Bob Hope/Bing Crosby "Road Movies." Musical numbers include such favorites as "Pennies from Heaven," "Misty," "Ain't It a Shame About Mame," "Like Someone in Love," and, of course, the Academy Award winning title song, "Swinging on a Star." *"A WINNER. YOU'LL HAVE A BALL!" - New York Post. "A dazzling, toe-tapping, finger-snapping delight!" - ABC Radio Network. "Johnny Burke wrote his songs with moonbeams!" - New York Times.* [3M, 4W]

❑ **THE MONOGAMIST by Christopher Kyle.** Infidelity and mid-life anxiety force a forty-something poet to reevaluate his 60s values in a late 80s world. *"THE BEST COMEDY OF THE SEASON. Trenchant, dark and jagged. Newcomer Christopher Kyle is a playwright whose social satire comes with a nasty, ripping edge - Molière by way of Joe Orton." - Variety. "By far the most stimulating playwright I've encountered in many a buffaloed moon." - New York Magazine. "Smart, funny, articulate and wisely touched with rue...the script radiates a bright, bold energy." - The Village Voice.* [2M, 3W]

❑ **DURANG/DURANG by Christopher Durang.** These cutting parodies of *The Glass Menagerie* and *A Lie of the Mind*, along with the other short plays in the collection, prove once and for all that Christopher Durang is our theater's unequivocal master of outrageous comedy. *"The fine art of parody has returned to theater in a production you can sink your teeth and mind into, while also laughing like an idiot." - New York Times. "If you need a break from serious drama, the place to go is Christopher Durang's silly, funny, over-the-top sketches." - TheatreWeek.* [3M, 4W, flexible casting]

TODAY'S HOTTEST NEW PLAYS

❑ **THREE VIEWINGS by Jeffrey Hatcher.** Three comic-dramatic monologues, set in a midwestern funeral parlor, interweave as they explore the ways we grieve, remember, and move on. *"Finally, what we have been waiting for: a new, true, idiosyncratic voice in the theater. And don't tell me you hate monologues; you can't hate them more than I do. But these are much more: windows into the deep of each speaker's fascinating, paradoxical, unique soul, and windows out into a gallery of surrounding people, into hilarious and horrific coincidences and conjunctions, into the whole dirty but irresistible business of living in this damnable but spellbinding place we presume to call the world." - New York Magazine.* [1M, 2W]

❑ **HAVING OUR SAY by Emily Mann.** The Delany Sisters' Bestselling Memoir is now one of Broadway's Best-Loved Plays! Having lived over one hundred years apiece, Bessie and Sadie Delany have plenty to say, and their story is not simply African-American history or women's history...it is our history as a nation. *"The most provocative and entertaining family play to reach Broadway in a long time." - New York Times. "Fascinating, marvelous, moving and forceful." - Associated Press.* [2W]

❑ **THE YOUNG MAN FROM ATLANTA Winner of the 1995 Pulitzer Prize. by Horton Foote.** An older couple attempts to recover from the suicide death of their only son, but the menacing truth of why he died, and what a certain Young Man from Atlanta had to do with it, keeps them from the peace they so desperately need. *"Foote ladles on character and period nuances with a density unparalleled in any living playwright." - NY Newsday.* [5M, 4W]

❑ **SIMPATICO by Sam Shepard.** Years ago, two men organized a horse racing scam. Now, years later, the plot backfires against the ringleader when his partner decides to come out of hiding. *"Mr. Shepard writing at his distinctive, savage best." - New York Times.* [3M, 3W]

❑ **MOONLIGHT by Harold Pinter.** The love-hate relationship between a dying man and his family is the subject of Harold Pinter's first full-length play since *Betrayal*. *"Pinter works the language as a master pianist works the keyboard." - New York Post.* [4M, 2W, 1G]

❑ **SYLVIA by A.R. Gurney.** This romantic comedy, the funniest to come along in years, tells the story of a twenty-two year old marriage on the rocks, and of Sylvia, the dog who turns it all around. *"A delicious and dizzy new comedy." - New York Times. "FETCHING! I hope it runs longer than Cats!" - New York Daily News.* [2M, 2W]